DANNY NICHOLSON

Science for Primary Teachers

thinkbank
Education & Training

First published by Think Bank Ltd 2022

Copyright © 2022 by Danny Nicholson

All rights reserved. No part of this publication may be reproduced, stored or transmitted in any form or by any means, electronic, mechanical, photocopying, recording, scanning, or otherwise without written permission from the publisher. It is illegal to copy this book, post it to a website, or distribute it by any other means without permission.

Danny Nicholson asserts the moral right to be identified as the author of this work.

Danny Nicholson has no responsibility for the persistence or accuracy of URLs for external or third-party Internet Websites referred to in this publication and does not guarantee that any content on such Websites is, or will remain, accurate or appropriate.

First edition

This book was professionally typeset on Reedsy.
Find out more at reedsy.com

Contents

1	About this guide	1
2	Plants	4
	Identifying and Naming Plants	4
	Structure of a Plant	6
	What do plants need to stay alive?	8
	Plant Reproduction, Pollination	9
	Seed Dispersal	13
	Germinating Seeds	13
	Asexual Reproduction in Plants	15
	Useful Links	16
3	Living Things and Habitats	18
	Classifying Living Things – What makes something alive?	18
	Grouping Living Things	19
	Why is a mushroom not a plant?	20
	Carl Linnaeus and Classification	21
	Vertebrates and Invertebrates	21
	Classification and Keys	24
	Animal Life Cycles	26
	Observing Life Cycles	27
	How does a caterpillar turn into a butterfly?	28
	Human life cycles	28
	Habitats	29
	Animals at Risk	31
	Hunting for Minibeasts	31
	Useful Links	32

4	Evolution and Inheritance	34
	Adaptation	34
	Evolution and Natural Selection	37
	Useful Links	44
5	Animals Including Humans	46
	Basic Needs of Animals and Humans	46
	The Skeleton, Muscles and Movement	47
	Teeth	50
	Food and Digestion	52
	Food groups	55
	Food chains	56
	Heart and Circulatory System	59
	Breathing and Exercise	62
	Useful Links	64
6	Materials and their Properties	66
	Properties of Materials	66
	Linking properties to their uses	69
	Types of rocks and the rock cycle	70
	Soils	74
	States of Matter and particle theory	75
	Changing State	78
	The Water Cycle	80
	Physical Changes	81
	Chemical Changes	84
	Mixtures and Compounds	85
	Useful Links	86
7	Forces	89
	What are forces?	89
	"Seeing" the Forces	91
	Mass and Weight	92
	Moving objects	92
	Air resistance and friction	95
	Simple machines – gears, levers, pulleys	97

	Magnets	100
	Making a Magnet	101
	Useful Links	102
8	The Earth in Space	104
	Movement of the Earth, Sun and Moon	104
	How do we get day and night?	105
	How do the seasons change?	107
	Why do we get Seasons?	108
	Why do we get Moon Phases?	110
	Eclipses	112
	Stars, Planets, Galaxies	112
	The Solar System	113
	Useful Links	115
9	Electricity	117
	What is electricity?	117
	Conductors and Insulators	118
	Circuits	118
	Bulbs and Batteries	121
	Drawing Circuits	122
	Models and analogies in electricity	123
	Electrical Safety	126
	Where does electricity come from?	126
	Application of Electricity – things to make and do	127
	Useful Links	129
10	Light and Sound	131
	What is Light?	131
	Mirrors	133
	How do we get shadows and how do they change?	135
	Investigating Shadows	135
	What is Sound?	137
	Investigating Sound – changing pitch and volume	139
	How do we hear?	142
	Useful Links	143

11	What is Science and Working Scientifically?	145
	Science and the Scientific Method	145
	The Big Ideas in Science	147
	Working Scientifically Skills	149
	Types of Investigation	149
	Collecting and Presenting Data	151
	Useful Links	153
12	Planning a Science Lesson	155
13	Structuring a Science Course	159
14	Progression of Science ideas and content	163
15	Taking Science Outside of the Classroom	166
16	Dealing with Science Misconceptions	170
17	Questioning in Primary Science	173
18	Pupil Talk in Primary Science	178
19	Assessment in Primary Science	183
	Formative Assessment Techniques	185
20	Science and Computing/ICT	189
	Data Handling and ICT	192
	Simulations	196
21	Raising Interest and Challenging Stereotypes in Science	200

1

About this guide

The aim of this guide is to provide primary school teachers with the science subject knowledge they need to teach science with confidence.

Along with the science knowledge, it will also highlight opportunities and ideas for classroom activities you can do along with links to other resources and research that provide further information or support.

For more help and advice on teaching primary science visit www.sciencefix.co.uk

More Links

I've collated a load of websites and resources to support the teaching of science on Wakelet. They can be found at:

https://wakelet.com/@SCITT_Science_Resources_Primary4236
or scan this QR code with your phone:

YouTube Videos

A playlist of YouTube videos to support the teaching of science can be found here: https://www.youtube.com/playlist?list=PL4Xvr_xHjF0jLUGp-rjyP31MsVN6HIpFh

ABOUT THIS GUIDE

2

Plants

Identifying and Naming Plants

Studying the plants around us can stimulate an interest in nature and the local environment. It can also provide opportunities for taking science out of the classroom and into the real world.

Within the KS1 Science National Curriculum, there is a requirement for pupils to be able to identify some of the plants in your local environment. Most schools will have nearby trees which can be used for this.

Here are a few of the common trees you might find within your school grounds. They can be easily identified by their leaf shapes and by their fruits in the autumn.

Oak: The leaves of an oak tree are lobed and wavy. Usually, there are 5-7 lobes on each side of the leaf. In the autumn, these trees produce acorns.

Beech: The leaves of a beech tree are pointed ovals. There are 5-9 pairs of veins coming off a central vein. These trees also produce cob nuts.

Holly: Holly has shiny, glossy leaves with spines along the edge of the leaf. It is usually dark green on the top of the leaf and paler green on the bottom. They produce red berries.

Sycamore: The sycamore has a large leaf with 5 distinct lobes. Each lobe has a vein which radiates from the stem. The edge of the leaf is toothed. These produce winged seeds that spin round like helicopters when they fall.

Horse Chestnut: The horse chestnut has a large compound leaf. This kind of leaf is made up of 5-7 smaller leaflets all coming from a single stem. The leaflets are narrow at the base and get broader towards the tip. Each leaflet has a prominent central vein. These trees produce conkers.

Silver Birch: The leaves of a silver birch are roughly triangular with round corners. The edge of the leaf is serrated. The bark of the tree is white or silver with black streaks.

Oak	Beech	Holly
Sycamore	Horse Chestnut	Silver Birch

Comprehensive guides and keys to identify common British plants can be easily found online such as the Nature Detectives Spotters Guides: http://www.treetoolsforschools.org.uk/activities/pdfs/pdf_leaf_spotter_sheet.pdf

You can also get apps for your phone that will try and identify most plants and trees from a photograph of the leaf or a flower such as LeafSnap,

PlantSnap or even Google Lens.

Remember: Trees Don't Move!

If you're worried about teaching this, the important thing to realise is that trees do not migrate! The trees you find in your school will stay the same for many years. Make a labelled plan of the trees around your school, keep it handy, and you'll be able to use it year after year.

Deciduous or Evergreen?

Trees and shrubs can be broadly grouped into those that are deciduous or those that are evergreen. Deciduous plants lose their leaves seasonally, usually before the winter or dry season. Water is lost from the leaves so losing the leaves allows the plant to conserve water. Common deciduous trees include oak, horse chestnut and sycamore.

Evergreen plants keep their leaves throughout the year. An evergreen plant gradually loses and replaces leaves all the time, there is no point in the year where it has no leaves. Evergreens include holly as well as most species of conifer tree such as spruce, cedar and pine.

Structure of a Plant

So, what exactly is a plant? This is a question that many pupils, (and some adults) find difficult. Take a minute and think, How would you describe a plant?

Young pupils often describe plants as having flowers with coloured petals, green leaves and a stem. Some will also think of the flower as being the whole plant. There are many plants that pupils might not immediately think of as plants since they don't have flowers such as mosses and ferns. To add to the confusion, they may have heard their parents in the garden differentiating between plants and weeds, pupils might think that there is a difference between the two.

In general plants are green due to the presence of chlorophyll within their cells. They are able to make their own food using light energy from the sun. The obvious plants that pupils will know about include trees, shrubs and grasses. There are many plants that pupils might not immediately think of as plants since they don't have flowers, this includes plants such as mosses and ferns.

Pupils will often think that mushrooms and toadstools are plants, but these do not have chlorophyll and can't make their own food. So they are in their own kingdom, called Fungi.

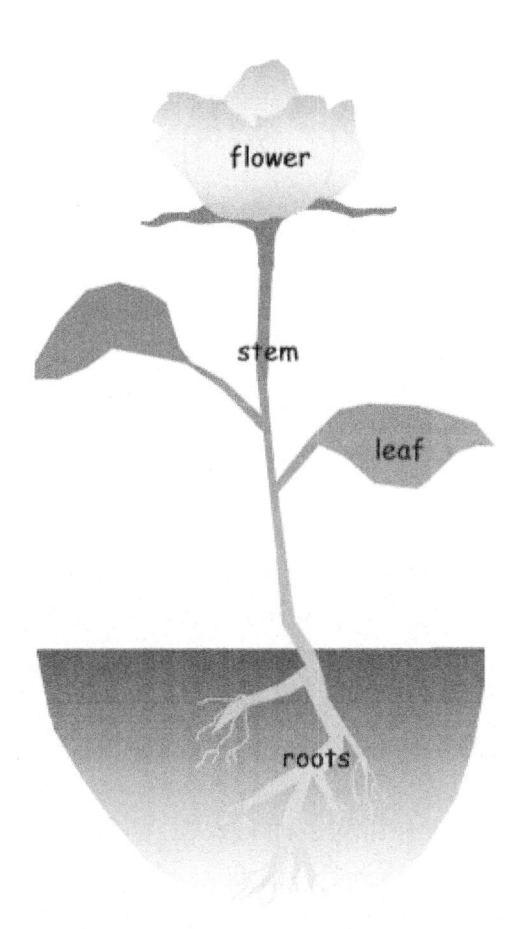

Parts of a Plant

The four key organs of a plant are the roots, stem, leaves and flowers. This video explains more: https://youtu.be/bLhTgTwbYMI

Roots: The roots absorb water and nutrients and store these for the plant. The roots also anchor the plant in the ground and prevent it from falling over.

Stem: The role of the stem is to transport water and minerals from the roots up to the leaves and flower. It also transports food away from the leaves to the rest of the plant. The stem also supports the plant, keeping it upright.

Leaves: The leaves contain chlorophyll and are responsible for the process of photosynthesis in green plants, where the plant makes its food.

Flower: The part of a plant responsible for reproduction. They contain eggs and make pollen. Some flowers are bright and colourful to attract insects to spread their pollen. Other flowers are less attractive and dump their pollen onto the wind to float through the air.

What do plants need to stay alive?

The most important things that plants need to stay healthy are **sunlight, warmth, water and air (carbon dioxide and oxygen)**. Sunlight provides the energy for photosynthesis, converting the carbon dioxide and water into glucose, which the plant uses as food. Plants obtain the carbon dioxide from the air around them and the water from the soil.

Like all other living things, plants also need oxygen, since they need to respire the glucose they produce within all their cells. This releases energy and allows the plants to carry out all the things it needs to do to stay alive.

Plants do not actually need soil to stay healthy. They can be grown in water with added minerals and nutrients, and this is called hydroponics. Many industrial greenhouses use this, and it has even been used to grow plants in space on the International Space Station!

Watch this video to learn more: https://youtu.be/_RXVhiUnTA8

Pupils can carry out simple experiments to see how plants grow in different conditions. Place plants in warm/cold and light/dark places and give plants different amounts of water and fertilizers to see what happens. These experiments can run over several weeks.

Misconceptions

A lot of pupils think that plants get their food from the soil. After all, we often talk about fertilizer as "plant food". It's true that a plant needs other chemicals such as magnesium and nitrates to make proteins and chlorophyll, these are not classed as food in the scientific sense of the word. "Food" is something that supplies a living thing with energy. For plants this is glucose, which they make themselves via the process known as photosynthesis.

However, in everyday use, the word "food" means something that a living thing takes in to give it nourishment. In this case, plants could be said to get some of their food from the soil.

Plant Reproduction, Pollination

How does a flower become a fruit? If you're a gardener, you'll already know this. But for many of us, especially pupils, this link is hard to visualise.

To understand what's going on when a plant reproduces, we need to take a close look at a flower.

Flowers contain the parts a plant needs to reproduce. Most plants have both male and female reproductive organs. Flowers have brightly coloured petals and a nice smell which attract insects. They often produce a sweet liquid called nectar to make it worthwhile for the insects to visit.

The male part of a flower is called the stamen. They are made of thin hairs called filaments, with a bulbous end called the anther. The anthers produce the pollen.

Pollen grains are as tiny as specks of dust, and they contain the male genetic material – half the information needed to make a whole new plant.

The female parts of the plant are called the Carpel (or pistil). They are made up of the stigma, style and ovary. Inside the ovary are tiny eggs which also contain half the information needed to make a new plant.

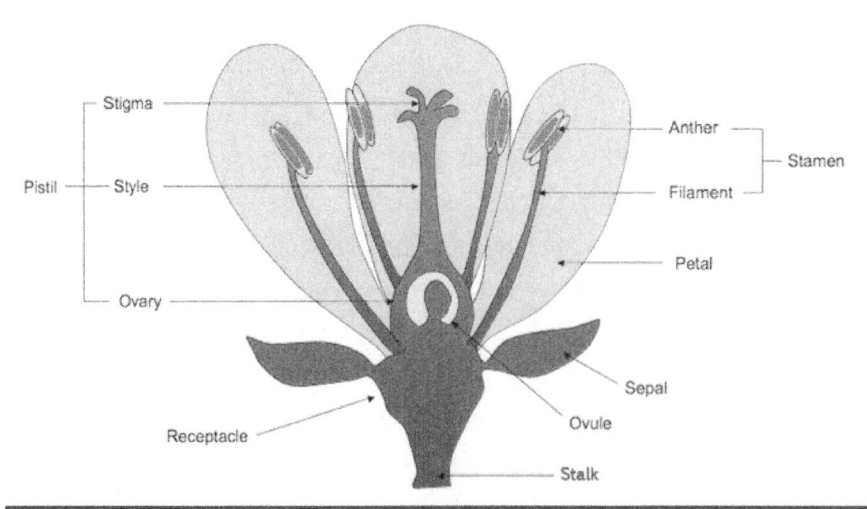

Parts of a flower

Pollination

The transfer of pollen, from an anther to a stigma, is called pollination. The pollen travels from the anther of one flower, and then eventually lands on the stigma of another flower. This can be carried out by insects, or by the wind.

This video explains more: https://youtu.be/nTVOH8-xb1I

Once the pollen has landed on the stigma, it grows a tube down the style to the ovary where it joins with the egg to fertilise it. The egg now has a complete set of genetic information needed to make a new plant.

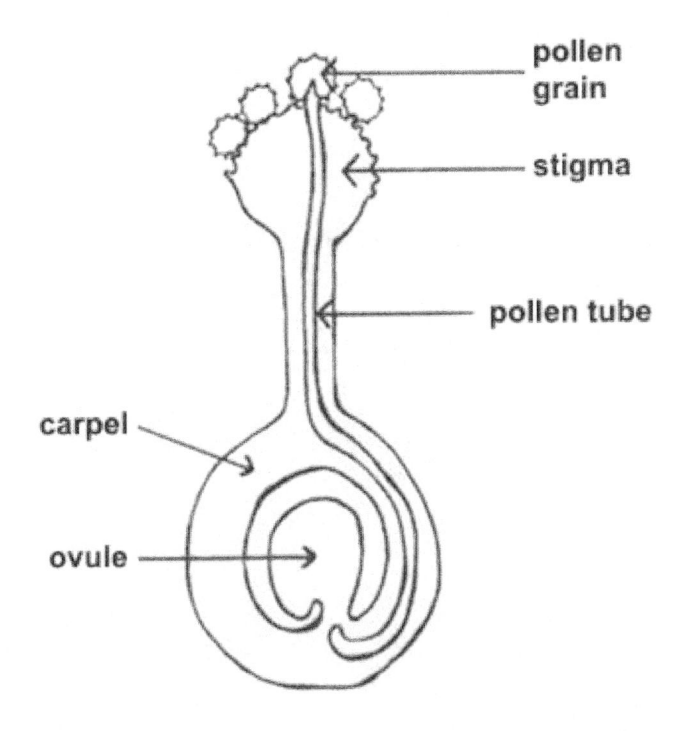

Pollination vs Fertilisation

There is often confusion between the process of pollination and fertilisation. Although they are closely linked, they are two separate processes. Pollination is the process by which the pollen gets from one flower to another. Once the pollen on the other flower it can then fertilise the ovule. The pollen joins with the ovule to create a, embryo that develops into a seed. One grain of pollen and one ovule is needed for each seed that is produced.

Fruits

Once fertilised, the ovary swells up. The eggs develop into seeds and the ovary develops into a fruit. The petals fall off. Next time you eat an apple, take a look at the bottom. You can still see the remains of the flower at the very end.

When you're eating a strawberry, an apple or even a courgette or pumpkin, you are eating what used to be the ovary of the flower. All of these are technically fruits.

A common mistake is that the word "fruit" is used to refer only to sweet-tasting plant products like apples, oranges and bananas. However, the botanical definition of fruit – the ripened ovaries of a flowering plant – encompasses many types of vegetables as well, such as tomato, cucumber, peas, beans and peppers.

Not only does the fruit protect the seeds inside, but it also attracts animals. Typically, animals eat the fruit and disperse the seeds in their droppings. Some fruits dry and split open to scatter the seeds.

Seed Dispersal

Plants **disperse** their seeds in lots of different ways. Some seeds are **transported** by the wind and have adapted their shape to float, glide or spin through the air.

Plants growing near a river may use the flowing water to transport their seeds.

Some seed pods are designed to **explode** and throw the seeds a good distance from the parent plant.

Many plants also use animals to **carry** their seeds. This type of seed may have handy hooks which attach to an animal's fur. As mentioned earlier, some plants might make tasty fruit to enclose the seeds, which **attract** animals to eat them.

Seed Dispersal: https://youtu.be/aC3pQ9RU9YA

Maddie Moate: How do seeds get around? https://youtu.be/nJAbo-F6tO4

Germinating Seeds

Germination is when a seed starts to grow into a new plant. Seeds don't always start growing right away. They need the right conditions to germinate.

Seeds need water to turn their stored food into energy to let them to grow. Oxygen from the air is also essential. And seeds will only germinate at the right temperature.

It is important to remember that **seeds do not need light to germinate.** Seeds that are germinated in the dark grow tall and thin since they "think" they are deeper underground and are trying to quickly get to the surface.

Most seeds germinate at around room temperature, so those dispersed in winter will wait for the warmer spring before they start to grow. Surprisingly, there are some seeds that need the extreme heat of a forest fire, whilst others prefer it just above freezing.

After germination has occurred, a small root, called the taproot, grows into the soil. Next, a small shoot sprouts. This grows up towards the light where it quickly develops its first two leaves so the plant can start making food through photosynthesis.

The seed has grown into a seedling. If the seedling is to survive it needs light, carbon dioxide and water. These are the vital ingredients for photosynthesis, which will give the young plant all the energy it needs to grow into an adult.

Germinating Cress

Cress is often grown in the classroom because it germinates really quickly. You can easily sow it on damp cotton wool or a paper towel. In the photo below, the cress on the left was put in a dark cupboard whilst the cress on the right was left in the light. The cress grows tall and thin because it is trying to find the light. Once out in the light it will turn darker green and grow normally.

Don't just grow cress every year. Try some other seeds as well such as mustard, sunflowers, broad beans and brassica. See the SAPS guides for more ideas https://www.saps.org.uk/primary/teaching-resources/1376-primary-bookle-4-living-processes-and-what-plants-need-to-grow

Asexual Reproduction in Plants

Living things are able to reproduce in two different ways - **sexual reproduction** and **asexual reproduction**.

In plants, sexual reproduction involves pollen from one flower fertilising the egg of another to produce a seed.

In asexual reproduction, only one parent is needed, and the offspring are exact copies. Some plants, like potatoes, produce tubers. These sit under the soil and develop into new plants next year. Some plants, like strawberries, grow runners which give rise to new plants. Some plants produce bulbs, like daffodils and tulips.

You can also take cuttings of plants. It is possible to take just a leaf from a plant such as geranium, plant it in a pot and it will grow roots (often a special hormone powder is needed to stimulate the growth).

https://www.bbc.co.uk/bitesize/topics/zxfrwmn/articles/z7jk8xs

Useful Links

Allen, M., (2016). The Best Ways to Teach Primary Science. Open University Press. **Chapter 3 – Plants**.

BBC Teach: Plants : https://www.bbc.co.uk/programmes/articles/Mf5rhb TkHLZ3fbJzScyDvC/primary-science-plants

Kew Gardens: Endeavour Plant Resources: https://endeavour.kew.org/home

Kew Gardens: Learning at Home: https://www.kew.org/learning/learning-at-home

Royal Horticultural Society: Campaign for School Gardening https://schoolgardening.rhs.org.uk/home

Science and Plants for Schools. Primary Booklet 4: Living Processes and What Plants Need to Grow https://www.saps.org.uk/primary/teaching-resources/1376-primary-bookle-4-living-processes-and-what-plants-need-to-grow

Science and Plants for Schools. Primary Booklet 1: Parts of a Plant and Their Function. https://www.saps.org.uk/primary/teaching-resources/1373-primary-booklet-1-parts-of-a-plant-and-their-functions

Science and Plants for Schools. Primary Booklet 5: Grouping and Classification https://www.saps.org.uk/primary/teaching-resources/1377-primary-booklet-5-grouping-and-classification-2

STEM Learning: Plants https://www.stem.org.uk/resources/community/collection/12535/year-3-plants

Wellcome: Darwin's Lookouts https://www.stem.org.uk/elibrary/collection/4100

Woodland Trust Nature Detectives. Tree Tools for Schools http://www.treetoolsforschools.org.uk/activitymenu/?cat=tree_id

3

Living Things and Habitats

Classifying Living Things – What makes something alive?

It's a big question: "What makes something alive?". As far as we know right now, our planet is the only one in the universe which has life on it. But if we do eventually travel to distant planets or moons, how will we know if we've discovered life? What will it look like?

Take a look outside if you can. Can you see any other living things, like trees or birds? How do you know they're alive? What are the characteristics of a living thing?

Pupils are often confused about what makes something a living thing. Something that moves fast that they can interact with such as a family pet is definitely alive. Something slow moving such as a bush or a daffodil may not be considered to be alive. Toys that move such as a toy robot could be mistaken for a living thing.

Characteristics of Living things

All living organisms have the potential to do these 7 things:

- **M**ovement

- **R**espiration
- **S**ensing
- **G**rowth
- **R**eproduction
- **E**xcretion
- **N**utrition (feeding)

It might not always be obvious that they are doing them, plants may not move very much and not everything might reproduce, but the potential is there.

A simple mnemonic to help you remember them is "**MRS GREN**".

There can also be confusion between things that were once living and are now no longer alive, such as wood, and something which has never been alive such as stone. It can help to try and track back to where that material came from. Wood was once part of a tree, but a stone has never been part of a living thing. Chalk is made from tiny animal shells, so it can be classed as dead.

Grouping Living Things

Kingdoms

All living things can be divided into five **kingdoms**, which depend on certain characteristics. The main characteristic is what their cells look like.

The 3 main kingdoms to consider at primary level are:

Animals: Any multicellular organism that feeds on plants or other animals.

Plants: A living organism that is able to make its own food by the process of photosynthesis.

Fungi: A group of organisms that include microorganisms like yeast and moulds. Fungi play an important role in decomposing plant and animal matter. Examples of fungi include athlete's foot, ringworm, mushrooms and toadstools.

As a simple rule – if it's green and can make its own food using sunlight then it's a plant. If it can move around and eats plants or animals then it's an animal. Fungi mainly eat dead and decaying animal and plant material.

The other kingdoms you might consider are:

Prokaryotes: A simple single-celled organism without a nucleus. Prokaryotes include **bacteria** and blue-green algae.

Protoctista: A group of microorganisms that either have one cell or many cells, but no specialist tissues. Protists include amoeba and protozoa.

Why is a mushroom not a plant?

Pupils often think that mushrooms are plants since they have roots and are grown in the ground. But if you look at a mushroom you will see that it's not green.

Without the green pigment chlorophyll, a fungus is unable to manufacture food from sunlight. Instead, fungi absorb their nutrients from plants or animals.

Carl Linnaeus and Classification

The modern classification system was started by Carl Linnaeus in the 18th Century. He originally only classified things as animals or plants.

Linnaeus proposed placing living things into progressively smaller and smaller groups. These are:

Kingdom, Phylum, Class, Order, Family, Genus, Species.

So, for us as human beings, our classification would look like:

Kingdom: Animal

Phylum: Vertebrate

Class: Mammal

Order: Primate

Family: Hominid

Genus: Homo

Species: Homo sapiens

Watch video: Naming Business https://youtu.be/vbofn9ROkGM

Vertebrates and Invertebrates

It's thought that there are roughly 8.7 million different species of living thing on Earth, and that around 1 to 2 million of these are animal species. How do we classify and organise all these animals? Initially it all comes down to whether they have a backbone or not.

We can begin by taking a look at whether an animal has a backbone or not. The earliest creatures had no backbone (or any internal skeleton), this was something that evolved later.

Invertebrates

Animals that have no backbone are known as **Invertebrates**. Some invertebrates, such as insects and crustaceans, have a hard exoskeleton, while others, like jellyfish, are supported by water. Invertebrates are sub-divided into smaller groups according to similar features.

There are many groups of invertebrates, but the main ones to cover at a primary level include:

Insects: Have three body parts, six legs and two antennae. Includes bees, wasps, butterflies, ladybirds.

Arachnids: Usually have four pairs of legs and no antennae or wings. Includes spiders and scorpions.

Crustaceans: Have two body parts and two pairs of antennae. Includes woodlice, crabs and lobsters.

Molluscs: Have a soft body, may have a shell. Includes slugs, snails, barnacles, and octopus.

Myriapods: Have a long body with many segments and lots of legs. Includes centipedes and millipedes.

Worms: Have a long soft body with many segments and no legs. Includes earthworms, and lugworms.

These would be the kinds of invertebrates you might find in the school grounds on a minibeast hunt.

Vertebrates

Vertebrates are animals with bony spinal columns or backbones containing a spinal cord. They usually have a hard skull enclosing the brain and eyes.

Vertebrates are divided into 5 main groups – based on their features.

Watch this video which explains more https://youtu.be/ITrRMiQB8g4

The 5 vertebrate groups are:

Mammals: These have fur and are warm blooded. They give birth to live young which are initially fed by milk from the mother. The embryos develop inside a womb and are attached to the mother via an umbilical cord. They don't lay eggs. Examples of mammals include humans, dogs, elephants, whales and seals.

Birds: These have feathers and lay eggs with hard shells. They are warm-blooded and have wings and two legs. All modern birds have a beak and no teeth. Examples of birds include eagles, ostriches, sparrows, pigeons, penguins and puffins.

Fish: Fish live in water, breathe through gills, and have no limbs with digits. Fish are cold-blooded. Fish lay eggs, although some species store the eggs within the body, such as seahorses. Examples of fish include salmon, trout, goldfish and sharks.

Reptiles: Reptiles lay eggs, are cold-blooded and have four limbs. They have dry scaly skin and lay leathery eggs on land. Examples of reptiles include lizards, crocodiles, snakes and turtles.

Amphibians: Amphibians have slimy skin, lay jelly-like eggs, are cold-blooded and have four limbs. They are able to breathe both on land and underwater. Amphibians lay eggs in water. Examples of amphibians include frogs, toads, newts and salamanders.

Shark vs Whale: Similar but Different

Look at the images of the shark and the whale. In what ways are they the same? In what ways are they different?

Whales may be wrongly classified as fish since they look very similar to sharks. Unlike sharks, Whales are warm-blooded and give birth to live young which they feed with milk. Sharks are cold-blooded and lay eggs. Sharks can breathe underwater using gills, but whales have lungs and so they need to come to the surface to breathe.

A whale is a mammal, while a shark is a fish. In evolutionary terms, whales are descended from land mammals that spent more and more time in the water and eventually evolved to cope with their new **environment**. This involved developing a streamlined shape and fins/flippers, ending up with a body plan very similar to a fish like a shark.

Classification and Keys

Classification keys are a means of identifying an unknown organism based on their distinct features. They require answering a series of questions about the organism's physical characteristics. The answers will either branch off to another question or will identify your unknown organism. The production of a classification key requires the author to identify sufficient key features of a known, previously named, organism to distinguish it from other organisms.

Within the Working Scientifically requirements, Lower KS2 pupils are required to be able to make use of ready-made keys. In Upper KS2 they should be able to use and develop their own keys.

Making a Key

When making a key, it is important to remind the pupils that the questions must be answerable with a yes or a no. You could introduce the idea by playing "20 questions" in pairs. One child thinks of an object and the other child has to ask questions which can only have a yes/no answer to guess what the object is. The board game "Guess Who" is also a great way to introduce this idea.

As well as creating keys for living things, pupils could start by making keys for types of biscuit or maybe characters from their favourite films or computer games. Animal finger puppets also work well, this video explains more: https://youtu.be/21wpERewkmI

Branching Databases

Check your school computers for any software that can be used to create branching databases. These can be used to create identification keys for different living things.

Pupils can also use software such as PowerPoint or Google Slides to make a key in the form of non-linear presentations. Using Yes/No buttons with hyperlinks to different pages in the presentation, pupils could make their own keys.

So, you can see Keys are a very useful tool for identifying living things. Spend time allowing pupils to use ready-made ones, and then have them create their own.

Task: Get a packet of liquorice allsorts or a tub of mixed sweets. Pick out 6 different sweets. Make a branching classification key for the sweets to identify each one. Each question should have a yes/no answer. You can find a guide to making a key here: https://www.bbc.co.uk/bitesize/topics/zxjj6sg/articles/z9cbcwx

Animal Life Cycles

Why do the babies of some animals look like miniature versions of their parents, whilst others look totally different? It's all down to their life cycle.

All living things go through a series of developmental stages known as a life cycle. For most plants and animals, the cycle begins when an ovum (egg cell) is fertilised by a sperm (male sex cell). As the organism's cells multiply, it grows and matures into adulthood. At this point the organism is able to reproduce, and the cycle continues with the next generation.

While the offspring of some organisms are simply smaller and less developed versions of the adult, others, including butterflies, frogs and ladybirds, undergo metamorphosis. Some life cycles are very short, with organisms developing from fertilisation to adulthood to reproduction in a matter of days or weeks. Other life cycles, such as that of the oak tree, can run for decades or even hundreds of years

Pupils often think of an egg as the "start" of a life cycle. In fact, since the different stages repeat in a continuous cycle, there is no start. However, it could be said that each individual organism starts life as a fertilised egg

Sex and Fertilisation

Within Primary Science, you should only cover fertilisation in animals, at the level of "sperm plus egg equals baby". Reproduction in humans, including sex and relationships, should be kept to Relationships and Sex Education (RSE or PSHE) lessons, and parents are usually notified about this. Ask in your school about their sex education policy

It is not necessary for the pupils to understand about genes or DNA. Explain that an egg and a sperm each contains half of the information needed to make a new living thing. When a sperm meets and joins with an egg that there is enough information to produce offspring. The egg and sperm then start to grow and develop into the animal

Metamorphosis

Metamorphosis is a process in which an animal undergoes a significant transformation to become an adult. The juveniles look totally different to the adults

For amphibians, this means growing legs, developing lungs and losing their gills. Tadpoles gradually change into frogs

For insects, the changes can alter their entire body, including growing legs, wings, eyes and antennae. A caterpillar will spin a cocoon and then emerge as a butterfly

Observing Life Cycles

One of the challenges in teaching this topic area is that most life cycles take place over a long period of time, so they can't always be observed in the classroom. However, it may be possible to show the pupils some examples of different life cycle stages as a series of images, or as time-lapse videos, such as this one: https://youtu.be/zOgYFSvkqI

Some zoos and wildlife parks place webcams in nest boxes or enclosures so that visitors can watch the babies. If you have a school pond it may be possible to carefully observe frogspawn and tadpoles in the spring. Caterpillars can be brought into the classroom, allowing pupils to observe the life cycle stages from caterpillar to butterfly. Some companies loan out incubators to observe chicks hatching. Search for "ethical chick hatching" to find reputable companies that do this

How does a caterpillar turn into a butterfly?

After hatching from its egg, a butterfly spends the first part of its life as a caterpillar. This is the butterfly's larval stage. The caterpillar is an eating machine, munching its way through as many leaves as it can and getting bigger and bigger

One day the caterpillar stops eating and enters what is known as the pupa stage. It hangs upside down from a twig or leaf and sheds its skin to reveal a hard protective casing called a chrysalis

Amazing changes happen inside the chrysalis. The caterpillar releases special enzymes that break down almost all of its tissues, forming a sort of lumpy caterpillar soup! Special groups of cells then begin to form the adult body parts such as legs, wings, eyes and antennae

Once it has rebuilt its body, the adult butterfly emerges from the chrysalis. When it first appears, the wings are soft and folded against the body. It then pumps blood into the wings to expand them and make them useable. After a few hours the butterfly is able to fly in search of food and a mate

Human life cycles

Pupils should also consider the changes that take place as humans develop from babies to old age. This needs to be handled sensitively, particularly the discussion of adolescence

This video from BBC Bitesize explains more:
https://www.bbc.co.uk/bitesize/topics/zgssgk7/articles/z2msv4

"Teaching about puberty before pupils experience it is essential to ensure that pupils' physical, emotional and learning needs are met and that they have the correct information about how to take care of their bodies and keep themselves safe. Teaching about puberty is also considered a key safeguarding issue by Ofsted." (PSHE Association Guidance.)

There are opportunities to link the topic of human development to other subject areas such as religious education. Many religions have "coming of age" ceremonies at particular milestones in a child's life such as First Holy Communion and Confirmation or Bar and Bat Mitzvahs. They could also think about PEGI ratings in computer games and BBFC ratings for movies and why these age limits exist

There's a wide range of life cycles you can study, and if you like you can include great examples of different models for parental care such as midwife toads and seahorses or total lack of care such as coral or sea anemones

Habitats

Planet Earth is the only planet that we know of that can support life and we need to look after it and all the animals and plants that live in it. A full understanding of habitats and ecosystems allows us to appreciate how we can manage them and conserve the resources within them

A habitat is any part of the environment in which a community of organisms is found. A habitat must provide food, water, air (oxygen for respiration in all living things and carbon dioxide for photosynthesis in plants), warmth/shelter, light and a place to reproduce

A habitat may be as small as a single leaf or rock or as large as a rainforest or the ocean, depending on the organisms that live within it. There may be competition between the organisms in a habitat for the limited resources, but also some interdependence of the species that live there.

A **microhabitat** is a very small habitat, forming part of a much larger habitat. For example, underneath stones and logs in a woodland, or under the soil

Take a walk in the school grounds or the local area and ask the pupils to identify possible habitats or microhabitats. These do not necessarily have to include obvious habitats like fields, flowerbeds or hedges; for example, organisms may live in a drainpipe or under an upturned flowerpot.

Before exploring these habitats, ask the children to discuss what type of environment each provides, thinking specifically about whether it is light or dark, wet or dry, if it contains many plants or few, and the condition of the soil.

Encourage them to think about what types of organisms they might expect to find there. Ask the children to sketch the organisms they find in the different habitats they explore. Ensure the children take care to replace things like rocks, pots or leaves in their original positions, so that animals' habitats are not disturbed unnecessarily

Pupils will also have seen many different animals on television or in films. You could relate ecosystems and habitats to movies such as The Lion King, Madagascar, or Finding Nemo. Use the environments depicted in these stories to discuss the real relationships between the animals.

See also Food Chains, later in this guide

Misconceptions

Pupils sometimes find it difficult to distinguish between homes and habitats. It might help to explain to them that a "home" is a place of shelter for an organism where it might spend some time. A habitat must provide all the requirements for life to keep the organism alive.

They may consider a habitat as unchanging, whereas most habitats change considerably over time due to human involvement, changes in climate and seasonal variations

Children often think that ecosystems are simply a collection of animals and plants living independently. In fact everything interconnects, with each living thing relying on others to for survival. You could start to discuss this with the children by examining an individual animal they are familiar with and begin to look at the other animals and plants it interacts with. Asking questions helps to prompt the discussion, such as what does the animal eat? What eats it? What happens to its waste products?

Some children believe that ecosystems are static and never change when in reality they can change because of many reasons. Human activity has a major impact such as pollution, clearing forests, burning fossil fuels etc

Animals at Risk

Ask the children to find out about endangered animals such as the orang-utan, mountain gorilla or leatherback turtle. Children can produce a presentation, display or short film that explains why the animal is at risk and what is being done to save them.

The children could also research some recent natural and man-made disasters that have affected specific habitats, such as major oil spills, earthquakes or volcanic eruptions.

Hunting for Minibeasts

Minibeasts is a name given to the many types of invertebrate that can be found in any school grounds – these include insects, spiders, snails and small crustaceans such as woodlice.

Take a walk in the school grounds or the local area and ask the children to identify possible habitats. These do not necessarily have to include obvious habitats like fields, flowerbeds or hedges; for example, organisms may live in a drainpipe or under an upturned flowerpot.

Before going out and exploring these habitats, ask the children to discuss what type of environment each provides, thinking specifically about whether it is light or dark, wet or dry, if it contains many plants or few, and the condition of soil. Encourage them to think about what types of organisms they might expect to find there.

Simple equipment, such as soft brushes, pooters, hand lenses and clear containers with lids containing air holes, can be used to collect and study the minibeasts in greater detail, helping the children to become immersed in their environment. Have some simple identification keys on hand for the children to use to identify any animals found.

Ask the children to sketch the organisms they find in the different habitats they explore. Digital cameras could be used to take photographs or short videos of the animals they find.

Useful Links

BBC Bitesize – What are Classification Keys?
https://www.bbc.co.uk/bitesize/topics/zxjj6sg/articles/z9cbcw
BBC Bitesize: How do humans change during their lifetimes?
https://www.bbc.co.uk/bitesize/topics/zgssgk7/articles/z2msv4
DFE Guidance. Relationships Education (2021):
https://www.gov.uk/government/publications/relationships-education-relationships-and-sex-education-rse-and-health-education/relationships-education-primar
Ideas for teaching identification and classification in the primary classroom:
https://www.stem.org.uk/news-and-views/opinions/ideas-teaching-identification-and-classification-primary-classroo
Linnean Society: Who was Linnaeus
https://www.linnean.org/learning/who-was-linnaeu
Outside Classroom Boards Minibeasts Key:
https://www.outsideclassroomboards.co.uk/product.php/minibeast_key
Naming Business
https://youtu.be/vbofn9ROkG
Nicholson, D. (2020) Keys and Classification Using Finger Puppets
https://www.sciencefix.co.uk/2020/11/keys-and-classification-using-finger-puppets

RBKC Ecology Service: Minibeast Pack:
https://www.rbkc.gov.uk/PDF/Minbeasts%20pack.pd

RHS Minibeast Identification Key:
https://schoolgardening.rhs.org.uk/resources/info-sheet/mini-beast-identification-ke

RSPCA – What is a habitat:
https://education.rspca.org.uk/education/teachers/primary/lessonplans/habitats/whatisahabita

Teaching About Puberty:
https://healthyschoolscp.org.uk/pshe/puberty

Young People's Trust for the Environment – lesson plans
https://ypte.org.uk/lesson-plan

Young People's Trust for the Environment: Minibeast Guide
https://ypte.org.uk/factsheets/minibeasts/identifying-minibeast

4

Evolution and Inheritance

Adaptation

Why does a polar bear look different to a brown bear? What does it mean when we say a living thing has adapted to where it lives?

Think about a polar bear. What features does it have that helps it survive in the Arctic? It has a thick layer of blubber under the skin to insulate it, as well as thick fur. Its feet are large to stop it sinking into the snow, with large claws for gripping the ice and ripping apart its prey. Its white fur helps it camouflage and it has small ears to help reduce heat loss. We can say the polar bear has adapted to life in a very cold and snowy place like the Arctic.

Evolutionary adaptations are traits with a current functional role in the survival of an organism within its environment. These adaptations have evolved by means of selection. One mechanism of selection is natural selection, which we'll look at later.

How has a cactus adapted to living in the desert?

Like all living things, plants show adaptations to their environment. They have evolved modifications to allow them to survive and reproduce in a wide range of conditions. Desert plants have to survive in very dry conditions where it might be a very long time between periods of rain.

The cactus, like many desert plants, has deep roots to absorb as much water as it can. They also store water in their thick stems to survive months or even years without rain. When it does rain the stem can swell up dramatically with water. The stem is covered in a thick, waxy cuticle to minimise water loss.

The leaves of a cactus have rolled up into tiny spikes to prevent water loss, and also to stop animals from eating them to get at the water stored inside the cactus.

This means they present much less surface area to the dry atmosphere of the desert and so lose far less water. Of course, there is a downside in that photosynthesis is greatly reduced and so they grow very slowly.

History of Life on Earth

Although adaptation is a slow process, Planet Earth is 4.6 billion years old. The first life began in the seas around 3.6 billion years ago, which means there has been plenty of time for life to change and adapt leading to the huge variety of life we see today.

The earliest living things were single-celled creatures such as bacteria and algae. Gradually life became more complex and multicellular life began. Plants made the move to land around 420 million years ago, and it took about 280 million years before flowers evolved! The first amphibians left the water and headed to land roughly 370 million years ago.

Dinosaurs ruled the Earth for 180 million years until a large asteroid hit the planet 66 million years ago causing massive changes to the climate (Natural History Museum, undated). This death of the dinosaurs cleared the way for a small group of mammals to thrive once conditions returned to normal. They in turn evolved into primates and eventually into humans.

Human beings have only been around for a tiny fraction of the Earth's history, 200,000 years or so. If the entire history of the Earth was condensed into a 24-hour day we wouldn't appear until a few seconds before midnight.

The table shows the timeline for life on Earth. The timescales involved are all big numbers, and it is very hard to visualise the scale of it. You could convert the numbers into distances to produce a timeline running along a school corridor or chalk this out on the playground.

	Million years ago
Present Day	0
Modern Humans Appear (Homo Sapiens)	0.2
Last Ice Age	2.4
First Human-like animals appear	2.5
Dinosaurs wiped out by asteroid	66
First Flowering Plants	141
Birds appear	195
First dinosaurs and mammals	230
First Reptiles	340
First insects	360
First Amphibians	370
Plants appear on land	420
Cambrian Explosion - First Fish	530
Simple multicelled creatures appeared	700
Algae, fungi, single celled animals appear	2100
Life first begins with single celled creatures like bacteria	3,600

Evolution and Natural Selection

You've all heard of Charles Darwin, and probably the phrase "survival of the fittest". But what does that actually mean, and how does it explain the abundance of life on the planet?

Within a population, there is variation. All living things have slight differences to the others, based on the features they have inherited from their parents. Even siblings will be different. These differences can give some the edge over others.

The phrase "survival of the fittest" causes a lot of confusion. It doesn't mean that only the strongest survive. By "fittest", we mean the best suited to the environment. These will have a better chance of survival, and so will reach adulthood and be able to breed, passing their useful features on to the next generation.

Evolution by Natural Selection relies on a few basic points:

1. There is variation amongst individuals in a population. They are all slightly different.
2. This variation is passed from parents to their offspring.
3. There is competition for vital resources. Not every individual will survive to breed.
4. Those individuals best suited to their environment are more likely to survive and breed, passing their successful genes on to the next

generation.

This can explain how a brown bear evolved into a polar bear. As they moved North, bears that had more body fat, bigger paws, or paler fur would survive better in the cold, snowy conditions. This would give them an advantage over other bears, and they would survive to pass these characteristics on to the next generation. Over tens of thousands of years, the polar bear evolved as we know it today.

Selective Breeding

Humans are able to speed up evolution in animals and plants, making choices about which features they wish to develop and which they want to lose. In this way, farmers have selectively bred different varieties of cattle for better milk or meat production, or sheep for wool or meat. All the different types of brassica, such as broccoli, savoy cabbage, kohl rabi and kale, were all bred by humans out of a single species of wild cabbage.

Dog breeders have, over thousands of years of selective breeding produced all the varieties of dog, choosing different features like size, body shape and coat colour. It took 30,000 years to turn a wolf into a chihuahua. Well done, humanity for that one!

When teaching this, you can link this topic to the jobs that different dogs do, and why different dogs are best suited for these jobs.

Theory of Evolution through Natural Selection

A theory to a scientist means a different thing than it does to everyone else. In everyday use, a theory means a guess or a hunch. These theories are often unproven.

But in science, a theory is a well-accepted explanation for a phenomenon based on good evidence. A theory ties together all the facts and can even be used to make predictions.

There is a wealth of evidence that supports the theory of Evolution by

Natural Selection. This theory has been tested and scrutinised for over 150 years and has been supported by an overwhelming amount of evidence. Scientists can look at the fossil record of the changes in animals over time, changes in DNA and even observe evolution taking place in bacteria in the lab.

Watch this video, which summarises Darwin's theory of Evolution: https://youtu.be/BcpB_986wyk

Darwin and Wallace

Charles Darwin is credited with the theory of evolution by natural selection. He developed his theory in the late 1830s, following his observations of the natural world. During his time on the Galapagos Islands, Darwin collected specimens of the different species of finch living on the island. It wasn't until he returned to the UK that he studied these specimens and realised how important they were.

By noticing that finches on the different islands had beaks that were adapted to their environment and realizing that finches whose beaks weren't adapted wouldn't survive, Darwin was able to start working out his theory of evolution. Darwin was worried about the response to his theory, so he didn't publish for over 20 years.

But Darwin wasn't the only scientist working on evolution. At the same time, another English scientist called Alfred Russel Wallace had also been developing his theory of natural selection whilst travelling around Malaysia collecting animal specimens. In 1858 he wrote to Darwin outlining his ideas. This spurred Darwin into action, and they published a joint paper outlining the theory of evolution by natural selection. But whilst Darwin went on to capitalise on this idea, Wallace went back to travelling the world.

Darwin's famous book "The Origin of Species" was published in 1859 and it immediately became a best-seller. It caused significant controversy at the time, as it challenged the view that God had created all the different forms of life on Earth. It also implied that all living things shared a common ancestor, and that humans had evolved from apes. Many people at the time found this deeply distasteful and it caused quite a scandal.

Evolution Misconceptions

Evolution is a subject area that has many misconceptions. Evolution is an incredibly slow process that takes place over thousands or millions of years. It is not something that can be easily observed in the classroom. Pupils might believe that animals and plants have always looked the same and have never changed. Study an animal such as a horse and look at how it has changed and developed over time.

A harder misconception to tackle is that animals "want" to change, to achieve a goal. It is hard to avoid saying that an organism is "designed" for living in a particular environment whereas, in reality, the organism has slowly adapted over many generations. Try and use the word adapted instead of designed whenever talking about how organisms are suited to their habitat.

For a very good summary of some of the misconceptions surrounding Evolution, take a look at this page on Evolution for Primary Kids: https://evolutionforprimarykids.co.uk/common-misconceptions/

How did the giraffe get its long neck?

Like all other animals, the giraffes evolved through a process of natural selection. The ancestral giraffe had a much shorter neck. Giraffes that were born with slightly longer necks had an advantage over other giraffes and so would survive to breed.

There are a few different theories about what the advantage of a long neck could be. Darwin suggested that the giraffes with longer necks could reach higher leaves when feeding than other giraffes and so they were able to compete better for food. These giraffes would survive better and pass on their genes for longer necks to their offspring. This advantage in having longer necks eventually led to the modern giraffe that we see today.

A simple answer for children would be that a mutation that gave a giraffe a longer neck would let it reach more food than other giraffes, so it had a better chance of reaching adulthood and passing that gene on to its offspring.

Evidence for Evolution

Fossils are the remains of organisms preserved in the rocks. We are able to date fossils, and so they provide a record of what lived on Earth many millions of years ago. They show a gradual change in living things, from simple to more complex forms, and they also provide evidence for intermediate forms between different groups of organisms. For example, scientists can find fossils of lizards that gradually show more bird-like characteristics to show that birds evolved from dinosaurs.

We can also observe similarities between living organisms. For example, the skeletons of all mammals are remarkably similar and also not very different from those of birds and reptiles! In a similar way, the genes of closely related species are much more similar than those of very different ones, supporting the idea of common ancestry.

We can also see evolution in action, especially in those species that have short life cycles. We have observed insects becoming resistant to chemical insecticides, and squirrels evolving in response to climate change, for example.

Camouflage

Many animals have adapted different forms of camouflage to hide from predators. Some just match the colours of the environment around them, whilst some have adapted to look like sticks, twigs or even leaves. The practical below shows how camouflage can be an effective way to hide from predators.

An interesting example to look at is the peppered moth since this adapted to a change in its habitat within a relatively short time span, and at a time when humans could study it.

The majority of moths were light coloured, only a tiny proportion had the gene which made them dark coloured. The pollution from the industrial revolution coated the trees in soot and also killed the lichen often found on tree trunks. The light peppered moth was no longer able to camouflage itself on the tree trunks, and so became easy to spot by birds. There was now an advantage to being a dark moth, as they were harder to spot.

As a result, the dark moths were able to survive long enough to breed and pass on the dark gene to their offspring. Within 100 years, 98% of all peppered moths were dark. With the introduction of controls for pollution, the number of dark moths fell and light moths increased again.

Darwin's Finches

During his time on the Galapagos Islands, Darwin collected specimens of the different species of finch living on the island. It wasn't until he returned to the UK that he studied these specimens and realised how important they were.

By noticing that finches on the different islands had beaks that were adapted to their environment and realizing that finches whose beaks weren't adapted wouldn't survive, Darwin was able to start working out his theory of evolution. The Galapagos finches are a classic example of adaptive radiation. Their common ancestor arrived on the islands a few million years ago. Since then, a single species has evolved into different species that are adapted to fill different lifestyles.

See: https://www.nhm.ac.uk/schools/teaching-resources/galapagos-finches-show-beak-differences.html

If humans evolved from monkeys, why are there still monkeys?

A common misconception arises from the assumption that we have evolved from the chimpanzees and apes that you can see today. This is not true. We didn't evolve from chimps, but we share a common, monkey-like, ancestor that both humans and chimps evolved from.

So, Apes and chimps are our relatives, in the same way that you are related to your cousins or second cousins. In the same way that you share a grandparent with your cousin, or a great-grandparent with a second cousin.

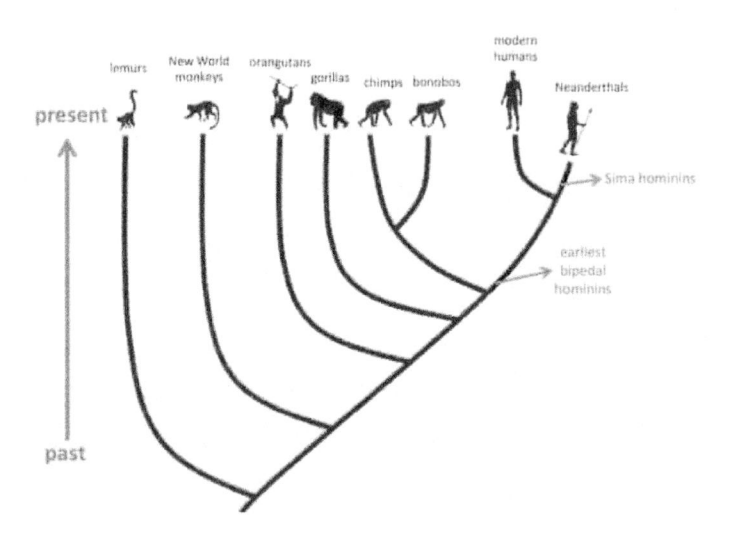

Useful Links

ASE: Mary Anning: A Fossil Hunter's Story: https://www.ase.org.uk/mary-anning-fossil-hunters-story

BBC Bitesize: What is Adaptation? https://www.bbc.co.uk/bitesize/topics/zvhhvcw/articles/zxg7y4j

BBC Teach: Charles Darwin https://www.bbc.co.uk/teach/charles-darwin-evolution-and-the-story-of-our-species/z7rvxyc

BBC Teach: Life and Work of Mary Anning: https://www.bbc.co.uk/programmes/p015gn89

Berkley Uni: Misconceptions About Evolution: https://evolution.berkeley.edu/teach-evolution/misconceptions-about-evolution/

Charles Darwin Trust: http://www.charlesdarwintrust.org/

Darwin's theory of evolution: https://www.livescience.com/474-controversy-evolution-works.html

Evolution for Primary Kids: https://evolutionforprimarykids.co.uk/

Le Page, M., (2008) Evolution, 24 Myths and Misconceptions. New Scientist. https://www.newscientist.com/article/dn13620-evolution-24-myths-and-misconceptions/

Natural History Museum: How an Asteroid Ended the Age of the Dinosaurs https://www.nhm.ac.uk/discover/how-an-asteroid-caused-extinction-of-dinosaurs.html

Natural History Museum: Evolution Teaching Resource. Spot the adaptations in Darwin's Finches https://www.nhm.ac.uk/schools/teaching-resources/galapagos-finches-show-beak-differences.html

Natural History Museum: When Whales Walked on 4 Legs https://www.nhm.ac.uk/discover/when-whales-walked-on-four-legs.html

Not just a theory: http://www.notjustatheory.com/

One Zoom Tree of Life Explorer: https://www.onezoom.org/

Primary Evolution. Teaching Evolution in Primary Schools: http://web.primaryevolution.com/

Peppered Moth Game: https://askabiologist.asu.edu/peppered-moths-game/play.html

What are evolutionary adaptations? https://youtu.be/kK2fIXlTesc

5

Animals Including Humans

Basic Needs of Animals and Humans

Humans and other animals can live just about anywhere on Earth, even in the coldest habitat of the Arctic. But no matter where we live, there are some things that humans and all animals cannot survive without. We call these things our basic needs. These are: Food, Water, Oxygen and shelter.

Food gives us energy, as well as other nutrients our bodies need. Different animals need different types and amounts of food. Most humans eat every few hours, while some snakes won't eat for weeks after consuming a large meal. We store excess food as fat – then break this down if food is scarce.

Water is needed for our bodies to work properly. Our bodies are about 50-70% water. We lose water through our urine and sweat so we need to top it up regularly. We can only survive a few days without drinking water.

Oxygen is needed for respiration. All animals need oxygen. We use it in respiration, the process of getting energy out of our food. This takes place inside every cell of our bodies. Animals living on land get oxygen from air, while fish have gills to absorb oxygen from water.

Shelter protects us from the environment. Animals couldn't survive without shelter from the environment. When the weather is bad many birds shelter in nests. Other animals shelter in underground burrows. While humans build houses.

The Skeleton, Muscles and Movement

Bones are very important – without them we wouldn't be able to do much at all. The adult human body is made up of 206 bones. Babies are born with nearly 300, but these start to fuse together as they get older.

All vertebrates, including humans, have a skeleton inside their bodies. This performs three very important roles:

Support – gives the body its structure. Allows us to stand upright.

Protection – some of our most important organs are protected by bones – such as the skull which protects the brain and the ribs which protect the heart and lungs.

Movement – muscles are attached to bones. The muscles make the bones move, which allows us to move around

Watch this BBC Bitesize Video to Learn more: https://www.bbc.co.uk/bitesize/clips/ztfnvcw

A **joint** is a place where two or more bones meet. This is usually somewhere obvious like a knee or elbow, but there are also joints between the bones in our spine and in our skull. There are many different types of joint that the pupils should be aware of: ball and socket (like the shoulder), hinge (like the knee), and immovable joints like those between the bones in our skull.

Tendons connect muscles to bones. Tendons work together with muscles to enable movement of the skeleton.

Ligaments connect bones together at joints. Ligaments protect joints by keeping them stable and restricting movement.

Muscles can only pull, they cannot push. A muscle contracts and gets shorter and this will pull on the bone and make it move. Muscles usually work in pairs – one contracts and pulls while the other one relaxes. Think about how your forearm moves at the elbow – the biceps muscles contract and lift your arm up. To lower your arm back, the biceps muscles relax and the triceps muscles contract and pull the arm down again.

Misconceptions

Pupils develop many different ideas about the bones and muscles in their bodies. They will probably be aware of the muscles in their arms and legs, as they use these often, but they might not realise that muscles are found all around the body. Ask them to think about how our eyes move, or how our mouth changes shape.

Some pupils may think that muscles are only used for actions like walking or throwing. They probably won't think of the heart or the tongue as a muscle. Pupils often think that muscles push rather than pull and will probably not be aware that muscles have to work in pairs to allow movement.

Pupils may not realise that bones are actually living tissue. (Caravita and Falchetti, 2005). They may know that milk is good for their bones and teeth but may not know that this is because it contains lots of calcium – a mineral needed for building and maintaining healthy bones and teeth.

Teaching about the skeleton

ANIMALS INCLUDING HUMANS

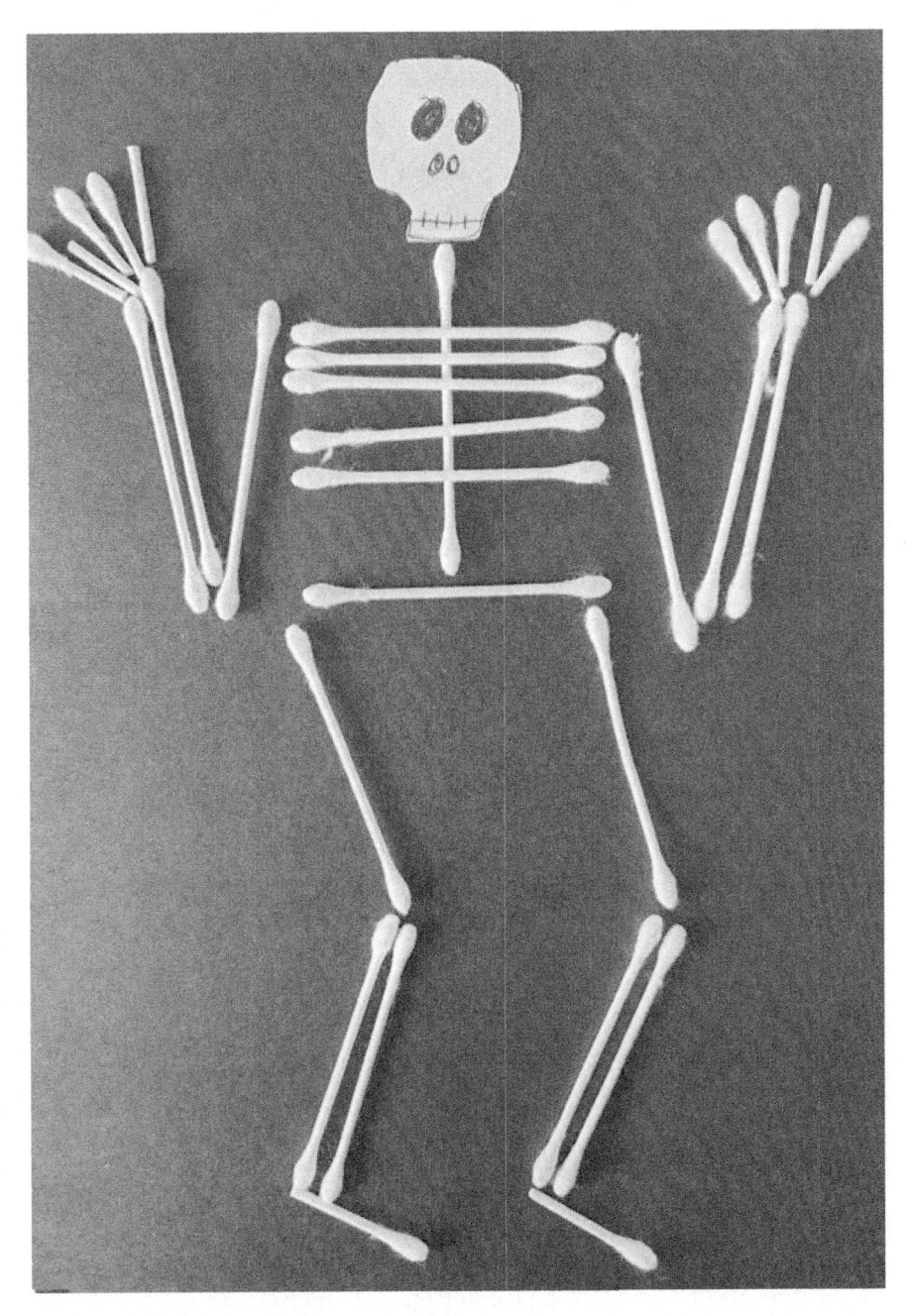

Provide the pupils with opportunities to handle real bones where possible. Leftover chicken bones from meals can be cleaned by boiling them for 40

minutes, then allowing them to cool. Scrub off any excess meat then sterilise with disinfectant. Leave to dry before use. As an investigation, the pupils could soak a chicken bone in different liquids for several days to see the effects. Acids like vinegar or cola will dissolve the calcium, leaving only the flexible cartilage.

Explore the skeleton (and the other organs) using a tool such as Zygote Body https://www.zygotebody.com/

You could build a skeleton from straws, pasta or cotton buds. Build a skeleton out of everyday items and add labels. See this twitter post from Mount Junior School for inspiration: https://twitter.com/mountoutdoor/status/1349363297271820289

You can also make a model hand to explore how the tendons in your arm make your fingers move. This guide explains more: https://www.sciencefix.co.uk/2019/07/make-a-model-hand-with-moving-fingers/

Cross-Curricular Links

There are good links to be made with PE, thinking about the muscles used for different sports – why does a sprinter look different to a high jumper or a shot putter, for example. They could also listen to different musical movements from The Carnival of the Animals suite by Saint-Saëns such as elephant or kangaroo and think about how the music reflects how the animals move. They could create their own dances in time to the music (https://en.wikipedia.org/wiki/The_Carnival_of_the_Animals)

Teeth

Typically, our mouths contain several different types of teeth, each with a different role.

Incisors: The teeth right at the front of our mouth. Humans have four on the top row of teeth and four on the bottom row. Incisors are used for biting into, cutting and chopping food.

Canines: The pointed teeth at the front of the mouth, either side of the incisors. Canine teeth help rip and tear food.

Molars: The wide flat teeth at the back of our mouth. These are used for grinding food.

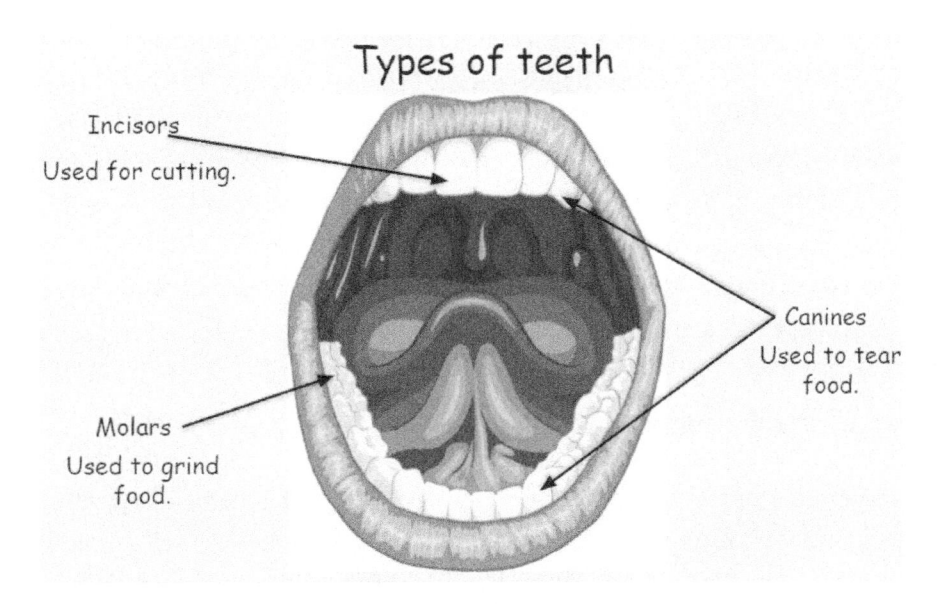

Types of teeth

Incisors
Used for cutting.

Canines
Used to tear food.

Molars
Used to grind food.

Herbivore vs Carnivore Teeth

Because of the different foods they eat, herbivore teeth have adapted differently to carnivore teeth. Pupils should look at a variety of different examples to compare.

In a carnivore such as a cat or a dog, the teeth have adapted to a life of eating meat. The molars at the back of the mouth are very sharp and slide over each other like a pair of scissors. This is ideal for ripping and cutting meat. Large canine teeth at the front help when biting and killing their prey. The incisors at the front are used in grasping prey and for tearing meat from bones.

In a herbivore such as a sheep or a cow, the teeth are very different. Plant material is very tough and needs a lot of chewing to break it up. Because of this, the back molars are wide and flat for grinding. In grass eaters, the top set of incisors has been replaced by a flat bony plate. Often the canine teeth are missing completely.

Things to Try

A classic investigation is to look at the effect of acids on teeth, using egg shells as stand-in for teeth. Read this guide for the instructions: https://www.sciencefix.co.uk/2020/01/how-liquids-affect-your-teeth-egg-shells-in-acid/

You could ask the pupils to look at different types of poo (no, really). You could make herbivore, carnivore and omnivore poo in advance (like this recipe: https://www.yac-uk.org/activity/make-and-excavate-archaeological-poo.) and see if they can work out which is which. Could link this to books like Poo in the Zoo or The Little Mole Who Knew it was None of his Business. Can the pupils identify what animal made the poo?

Food and Digestion

Have you stopped to consider exactly what happens to your dinner once you've eaten it? What does your body do with that sandwich after you've swallowed it? This section will look at the process of digestion and how you can model it with the pupils.

Pupils might already have their own words for parts of their digestive system, for example they might refer to the entire area as their tummy, stomach or maybe their belly. The stomach is actually a lot higher up than most of us think, it's just below the rib cage on the left. Think of the area that hurts when you get heartburn (which, to add to the confusion is nothing to do with your heart!)

Some very young pupils might believe that the digestive system is a tube that travels from their mouth goes to their stomach and no further (Allen, 2010). They might also think that food goes down one tube, and drink goes down another, hence food "going down the wrong hole".

Checking Understanding of Organs

To check their initial understanding of internal organs, you could give pupils outlines of the body and ask them to draw what they think it looks like inside them. (Andersson et al. 2020. Reiss & Tunnicliffe 2001) They could use flipchart paper and draw around each other to get an outline or chalk an outline on the playground.

Discuss with the pupils that there is a tube for food and drink together and a second tube for air that goes to our lungs. Explain that when we swallow the food and drink goes down into the stomach where it is all churned up.

What is Digestion?

The chemicals in our food are too big for our bodies to use. **Digestion** is the process by which our bodies break food down into very small pieces. Pieces that are so small that we would need a microscope to see them.

Special chemicals, called enzymes, work a bit like a pair of scissors. They chop up the long chemicals into much smaller pieces. These small chemicals can then be absorbed into the body and used to make other chemicals.

The Digestive System

Digestion is a complex body system with a number of components. Although pupils do not need to know all the details of digestion, they should be familiar with the basic organs and the order that food passes through them.

Mouth
Oesophagus
Liver
Stomach
Small Intestine
Large Intestine
Rectum

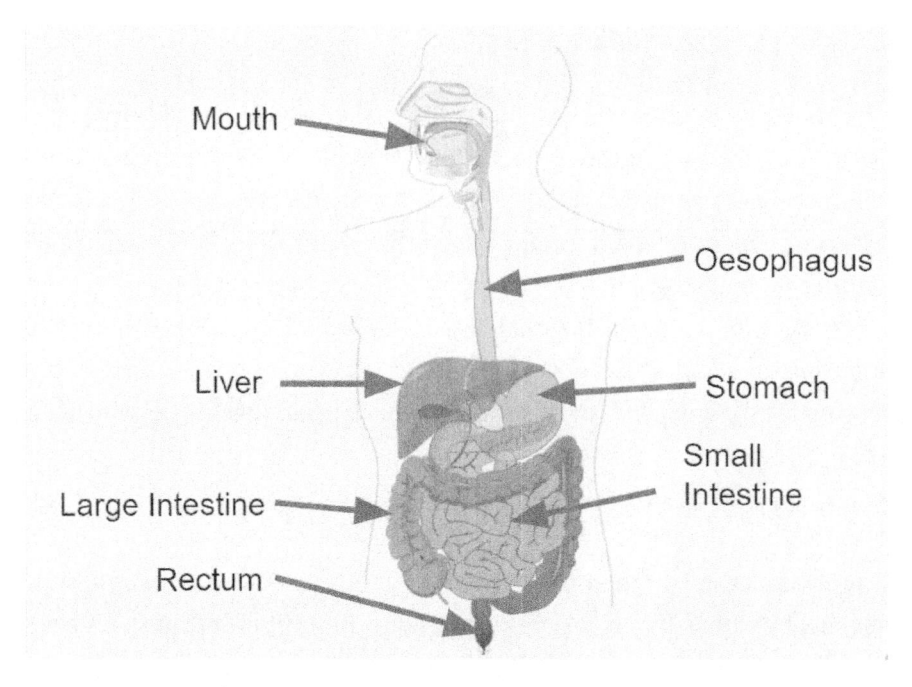

The main parts of the digestive system are:

- **Mouth** – Food is chewed and mixed with saliva. It starts to break down.
- **Teeth** – these help to break down the food into smaller chunks.
- When it is swallowed, it travels down a tube called the **oesophagus**
- **Stomach** – Food is mixed with digestive juices containing acid and enzymes which start to break the big chemicals down into smaller ones.
- **Small intestine** – Nutrients and useful chemicals and water are absorbed here and sent to the liver. Chemicals the body doesn't need keep passing through.
- **Liver** – The food absorbed from the small intestine is sent here. It's filtered and sent to the rest of the body through the bloodstream.
- **Large intestine** – Water is absorbed, and other waste products are added as it passes through.
- **Rectum** – Waste stays here and then leaves the body as poo when we go to the toilet.

You don't need to cover things like the gall bladder or pancreas, but it might come up in the lesson, particularly if any pupils are diabetic or know someone with a digestive problem.

As well as viewing the organs through a website such as Zygote Body (https://www.zygotebody.com), there are some interesting augmented reality apps such as Curiscope which superimpose the organs over a special t-shirt (see https://www.curiscope.co.uk/products/virtuali-tee).

Model the process of digestion

The video outlines a fun way to model the process of digestion using everyday items to see what happens to a cream cracker and banana.

Digestive System Demonstration: **https://youtu.be/3Awa5Wxko6I**

If you do this with a class, be sure to explain what each of the parts of the model represent and what is happening at each stage. For example, the stomach is the plastic bag. The stocking represents the small intestine etc.

Digestion is an important process, and it's fun to be able to explore how it works. If you like, you could also introduce scientists who studied digestion in rather gross ways like Lazzarro Spallanzani who used to swallow food on a string and regurgitate it or William Beaumont who studied a man who had been shot in the stomach, putting food through the hole then pulling it out later to see what had happened to it!

Food groups

Food is very important to all of us. There are many different types of food, and they all benefit us in different ways.

Unlike plants, animals cannot make their own food. They have to obtain their food by eating a plant or by eating an animal that has eaten a plant.

A common misconception is that we only need to eat food to give us energy (Allen, 2010). As well as the chemicals that give us energy, our food also contains other nutrients and chemicals that our bodies need to function properly – such as fats, proteins, vitamins and other minerals.

The food that we eat can be divided up into different groups. There are a few different ways of doing this but one way to classify the different food groups is as follows:

Group	Used for	Examples
Starchy Foods (Carbohydrates)	Energy	Bread, Potatoes, Pasta, Rice
Milk and Dairy	Calcium for strong bones and teeth	Milk, Cheese, Yoghurt
Fat and Sugar	Energy	Chocolate, Fizzy Drinks,
Protein	Growth, Building muscles	Fish, Eggs, Meat, Beans, Pulses
Fruit and Vegetables	Vitamins, Minerals and Fibre	Apples, Carrots, Bananas

Watch this video which explains more: https://youtu.be/L9ymkJK2QCU

It's important that we don't label foods as healthy or unhealthy. What we should be promoting is a balanced diet – with a good combination of all different foods. The Eatwell Plate is one example of a balanced diet. Pupils could look at the school's healthy food policy and make a survey of the meals served in the school canteen.

Food chains

Unlike plants, animals are unable to make their own food. They must rely on the food that has been made by plants. Some animals do this by eating plants. Some do this by eating other animals. And some do both.

Herbivores: Animals that eat only plants. They have specially adapted digestive systems that are well suited to digesting plant matter.

Carnivores: Animals that eat only meat. They are especially adapted for catching, killing and digesting other animals.

Omnivores: These animals have a diet which consists of both meat and plant material.

In Key Stage 1, pupils should consider what different animals need to stay alive, including food. They could link this to different pets they might have at home. Why wouldn't you give cat food to a guinea pig? This could also be linked to zoos – maybe discuss feeding time at the zoo and what the different animals might need to eat.

To show the feeding relationships between organisms we can draw a food chain. In this section we'll look at how to draw one correctly.

Although we call it a food chain, it's actually showing the flow of energy from one organism to the next. The flow of energy is represented by arrows in a diagram.

A simple food chain might look like this:

GRASS → RABBIT → FOX

Every food chain consists of producers and consumers.

Producers are (nearly always) plants that make their own food through photosynthesis.

Consumers are animals that obtain energy by eating plants or other animals that have eaten plants.

Green plants are able to convert energy from sunlight into food stores by the process of photosynthesis.

Animals gain energy by consuming these plants or by eating other animals that eat plants. Animals that eat other animals are called predators, and the animals they eat are called prey.

https://www.bbc.co.uk/bitesize/topics/zbnnb9q/articles/zwbtxsg

What do the arrows show?

Pupils often get confused with the arrows in a food chain. Many think that the arrow in the food chain means "eats" and draw the arrows in the wrong direction.

Take a look at the food chain above. Each arrow represents the flow of energy, from the plant to the rabbit to the fox. The pupils could think of it as showing that the grass "goes into" the rabbit and then the rabbit "goes into" the fox.

Print out photographs of the fox, rabbit and grass along with large arrows and create food chains running on the floor for them to explore. Explain what's happening as they walk along it.

Allen (2010) suggests using the Pacman rule, based on the video-game character. Pacman only munches in one direction, and his mouth can form the tip of each arrow.

From Allen (2010 p55) Misconceptions in Primary Science. Open University Press

Sometimes, the situation is more complicated than that shown in a food chain, the top carnivore eats more than one food and may well eat some of the things lower down the chain – this is why a food web is a better way to represent the relationships in an ecosystem, but this is probably something to look at in KS3.

Stacking food chains

Give each group of pupils several plastic or cardboard drinking cups. Ask them to draw individual animals and plants then cut out and stick one animal or plant onto the side of each upside-down cup. Write the name of the organism around the lip of the cup so that it can be seen when the cups are stacked.

Stack the cups in different combinations to make different food chains. Take photographs of each combination as a record. More details here: https://www.sciencefix.co.uk/2020/10/quick-science-idea-make-food-chains-with-stackable-cups/

Heart and Circulatory System

The heart is the pump that powers everything you do. Whether you're sleeping or running a marathon, constant beat of your heart keeps you alive. Let's find out more

   Your heart is a muscle whose only function is to pump blood around the body. It's about the size of your fist and is located slightly to the left of the centre of your chest, not over on the far left like some think. It's also not "heart shaped"!

The heart has two sides, and each side has two chambers, the atrium and ventricle. The blood enters the heart into the atria, then flows into the ventricles where it's then pumped out.

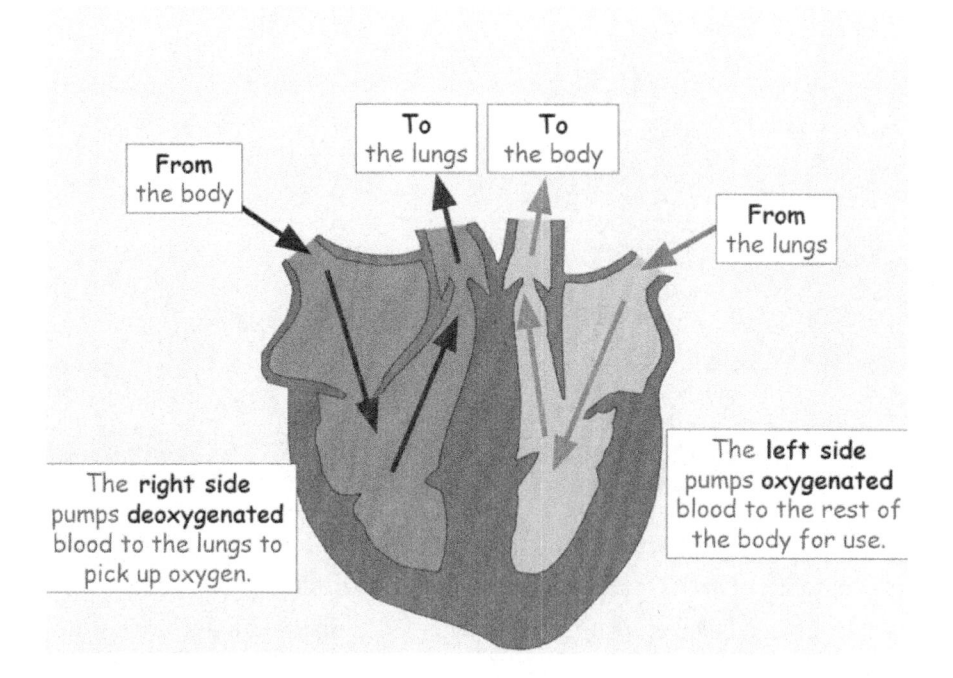

From the body

To the lungs

To the body

From the lungs

The **right side** pumps **deoxygenated** blood to the lungs to pick up oxygen.

The **left side** pumps **oxygenated** blood to the rest of the body for use.

The job of the right side of the heart is to receive blood from the body and pump it to the lungs where it picks up oxygen. The left side receives the oxygen-rich blood from the lungs and pumps it from the left ventricle out to the body via the aorta.

- The blood vessels that carry blood away from the heart are called **arteries**.
- The blood vessels that carry blood back to the heart are called **veins**.

As the blood moves out of the heart, the veins carry blood to all the different parts of the body, delivering oxygen and "fuel" powering everything from your brain to your muscles.

Blood is kept flowing in one direction by flaps of tissue in the heart, called **valves**. There are two pairs of valves, and they act like gates that can only be pushed open in one direction, stopping the blood moving backwards. It's the closing of the valves that make the characteristic sound of a heartbeat

Pupils could act out the movement of blood around the body on the playground. One area is the body, and one is the lungs, with the heart in the middle. Pupils could move in a figure of 8, from the body, through the heart to the lungs and back again. They could even carry tokens to represent oxygen which they collect at the lungs and deliver to the body, collecting a carbon dioxide token to bring back to the lungs.

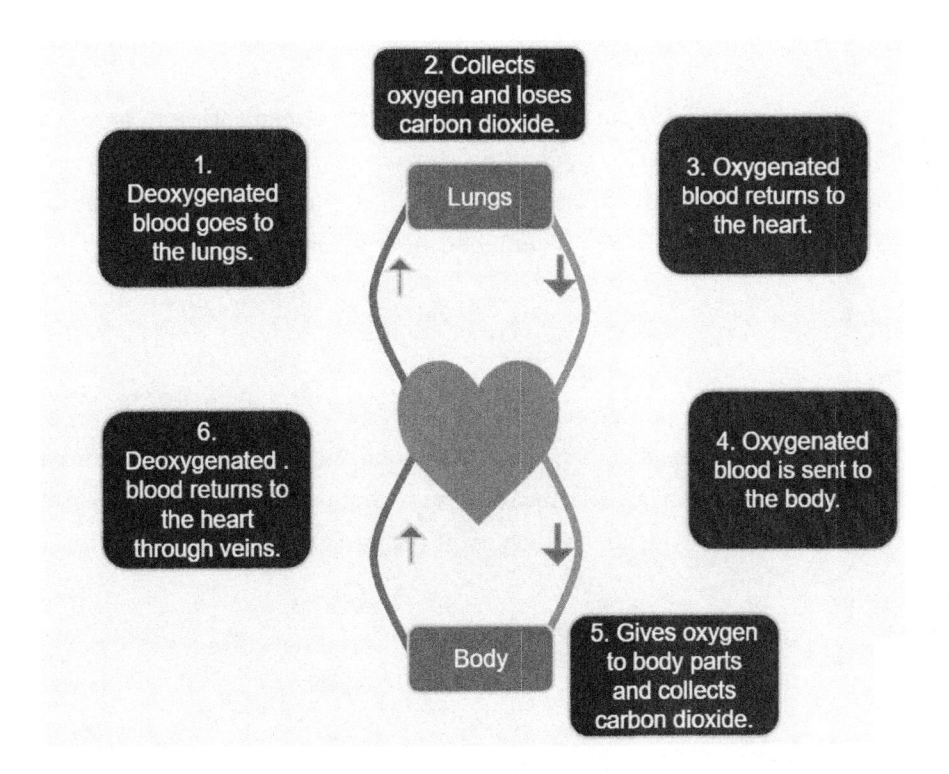

1. Deoxygenated blood goes to the lungs.
2. Collects oxygen and loses carbon dioxide.
3. Oxygenated blood returns to the heart.
4. Oxygenated blood is sent to the body.
5. Gives oxygen to body parts and collects carbon dioxide.
6. Deoxygenated blood returns to the heart through veins.

Blood is not blue

Its commonly believed that arterial blood is red and venous blood is blue. This is a really hard misconception to shake, and not helped by every heart diagram showing blood as red and blue. It's also sometimes thought that the reason why we don't see blue blood when we cut ourselves is because it becomes red as soon as it makes contact with the air (Allen 2010).

While it is true that your veins look blue when you look at them, this is due to the way they scatter and absorb red and blue light. The vein might look blue but the blood inside is still a dark red colour.

You can read more about this here: If Blood is Red, Why are veins blue? https://www.livescience.com/32212-if-blood-is-red-why-are-veins-blue.html

Breathing and Exercise

Every cell in your body carries out a process called **respiration** in order to release the energy it needs to function. Aerobic respiration requires oxygen and produces carbon dioxide as a waste product. We need to breathe in and out in order to get oxygen into our blood and the carbon dioxide out.

Breathing

Inside the lungs, oxygen diffuses into the blood and carbon dioxide diffuses out. The lungs have a huge surface area, very thin walls and are in very close contact with the blood, all of which helps the gases pass through quickly.

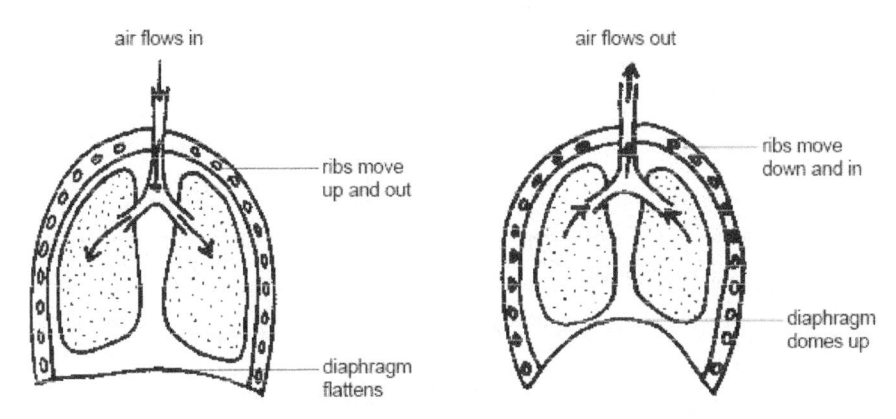

https://commons.wikimedia.org/wiki/File:Anatomy_and_physiology_of_ animals_Inspiration_%26_expiration.jpg

The process of breathing is called **ventilation** (not respiration). The lungs are surrounded by the rib cage and a sheet of muscle called the diaphragm. When you breathe in, the diaphragm contracts and moves downwards. At the same time, the muscles between the ribs contract and pull the ribcage up and out. This creates a greater volume in the chest, and therefore a lower pressure, which causes air to rush in. We call this **inhaling**.

Breathing out (**exhaling**) reverses these actions. The diaphragm rises up, the ribs fall, and the air is forced out of the lungs.

Air in vs Air Out

It's commonly said that we breathe in oxygen and breathe out carbon dioxide. This isn't true.

The air we breathe in is around 78% nitrogen, around 21% oxygen and a tiny amount of carbon dioxide (around 0.04%). The air we breathe out is about 4% carbon dioxide and 16% oxygen. The amount of nitrogen doesn't change. So, it is more correct to say that the air we breathe out has less oxygen and more carbon dioxide in it than the air we breathe in.

Effect of Exercise

As your body exercises, your muscles are respiring more because they need more energy. This means they require more oxygen as well as producing more carbon dioxide.

Your breathing rate will increase to get more oxygen into the blood and to remove more carbon dioxide. At the same time, the heart will pump faster to deliver more oxygen to the muscles and remove the carbon dioxide and get it back to the lungs.

Respiration can also occur in the absence of oxygen. This is called anaerobic respiration. Anaerobic respiration is less efficient than aerobic respiration and can only be used for short periods at a time. It produces lactic acid, which if allowed to build-up can cause cramp. This is why runners might get cramp or a stitch when running as the lactic acid builds up.

After exercise, it takes a while for the body to recover, until the demand for extra energy falls and any lactic acid is removed. Eventually heart rate and breathing returns to normal.

Measuring heart rate

Pupils can monitor their heart rate at rest as well as during and after exercise. Find a pulse point, either in the wrist or in the neck and count how many beats they detect in 15 seconds. You could also buy a heart rate monitor to do this, and many pupils might also have their own smart watches or fitness trackers which give an accurate heart rate.

Useful Links

Allen, M., (2010) Misconceptions in Primary Science. Open University Press.

Andersson, J., Löfgren, R., & Tibell, L., (2020) What's in the body? Pupil's annotated drawings, Journal of Biological Education, 54:2, 176-190, https://www.tandfonline.com/doi/full/10.1080/00219266.2019.1569082

Caravita, S. and Falchetti, E. (2005) 'Are Bones Alive?', Journal of Biological

Education, 39(4), pp. 163–170. https://www.tandfonline.com/doi/abs/10.1080/00219266.2005.9655990

How liquids affect your teeth: Egg Shells in Acid. https://www.sciencefix.co.uk/2020/01/how-liquids-affect-your-teeth-egg-shells-in-acid/

How do I check my pulse? https://www.nhs.uk/common-health-questions/accidents-first-aid-and-treatments/how-do-i-check-my-pulse/

Living Bones, Strong Bones. Nasa. https://www.nasa.gov/sites/default/files/atoms/files/bones_-_teacher.pdf

Live Science: (2012) If Blood is Red, Why are Veins Blue? https://www.livescience.com/32212-if-blood-is-red-why-are-veins-blue.html

Making Food Chains with Stackable Cups https://www.sciencefix.co.uk/2020/10/quick-science-idea-make-food-chains-with-stackable-cups/

Make and Excavate Archaeological Poo. https://www.yac-uk.org/activity/make-and-excavate-archaeological-poo

Nicholson, D (2019) Make a Model Digestive System https://www.sciencefix.co.uk/2019/05/make-a-digestive-system-model-using-crackers-and-bananas/

Reiss, M., & Tunnicliffe, S., (2001). Student's Understandings of Human Organs and Organ Systems. Research in Science Education. 31. 383-399. 10.1023/A:1013116228261.

The Eatwell Guide https://www.nhs.uk/live-well/eat-well/the-eatwell-guide/

Your Heart Rate: https://www.bhf.org.uk/informationsupport/how-a-healthy-heart-works/your-heart-rate

6

Materials and their Properties

Properties of Materials

Materials are a fundamental part of our life. All the "stuff" around us, and including us, is made of different types of material – from the clothes we wear, the houses we live in, even the air we breathe and the water we drink.

Pupils can be confused about the meaning of the word **material**. They might only have heard the word in the context of clothes and fabrics. A material is anything made from **matter**. Anything that is made from "stuff". Anything that physically occupies space and has mass.

Types of Material

There are many different types of material that the pupils may be familiar with as part of their everyday lives. This can include:

Metal: iron, aluminium, tin, gold and silver
Ceramic: bricks and tiles, pottery, china.
Glass: window glass, bottles and Pyrex.
Plastics: polystyrene, polythene.
Fibres: different fabrics in the clothes they wear plus string and rope.

Comparing and Grouping Materials

The appearance and properties of materials may be used to group or classify them and determine their appropriateness for a specific function.

For many pupils these classifications will be based on direct sensory experiences, how they feel, how they look. Allow them time to explore and sort a range of materials based on their own rules then suggest others they could use.

We can group them according to various properties:

- Texture: Is it rough or smooth, hard or soft?
- Flexibility. Can it bend or is it stiff?
- Waterproof: Does it allow water to pass through it; is it porous?
- Transparency: Is the material transparent, translucent or opaque?
- Magnetic: Is the material magnetic or not?
- Conductivity: Does it conduct or insulate heat and electricity? Does it feel cold when you touch it?

Give the pupils a range of materials and two hoops and ask them to sort the materials into different groups based on their own rules – are they shiny/dull, bendy/not bendy etc.

General Properties of Materials

Some of the general properties of the different groups of materials are described below. There will always be exceptions to these which can provide interesting discussion points.

Wood: Wood is strong but can be slightly flexible. It is a good insulator of heat and electricity.

Plastics: Plastics have many different properties. Some can be transparent whilst others can be translucent or opaque. Some are flexible while others can be quite stiff. They are good insulators of heat and electricity.

Glass: Glass is shiny and transparent. It is hard but inflexible and brittle. It is a good insulator of heat and electricity.

Metal: Metals are shiny, strong and usually hard. They are good conductors of heat and electricity. Some metals can be bendy, but others are not bendy.

Rock: In general rocks are hard and not very flexible. They are insulators of electricity

Object vs Material

At KS1, pupils should be able to distinguish between an object and the material from which it is made. For example, you could give them a variety of spoons; wooden, plastic and metal.

Pupils could investigate different types of ball. Look at balls made from different materials such as tennis balls, ping pong balls, squash balls and golf balls. How are they the same? How are they different? Could they investigate which ball is the bounciest?

To do: Read the "Grouping and Classifying Materials" pdf from the Royal Society of Chemistry https://edu.rsc.org/download?ac=14823. Think about how you could use some of these activities with a year 1 class.

Teaching Materials in the Early Years

In the early years, allow the pupils to explore the materials for themselves. The Sand Tray and Water tray provide lots of opportunities for structured and unstructured exploration of different materials. You don't need anything fancy, at a pinch a plastic storage crate will do the trick. Many accessories such as funnels, sponges and sieves can be picked up cheaply in Pound shops or similar.

Read these articles for some ideas:

Sand Table Science Ideas: https://www.sciencefix.co.uk/2019/04/early-years-sand-table-science-ideas/

Water Table Science Ideas: https://www.sciencefix.co.uk/2019/04/early-years-water-table-science-ideas/

Linking properties to their uses

Different materials behave in different ways, and it is these different properties that make them suitable for particular uses. When designing new structures, engineers will select materials that are best suited to the job – based on their strength, flexibility, density and many other properties.

This can be sometimes hard for the pupils to understand. They may start with cyclical ideas about the use of materials for different jobs, for example, we use rubber to make wellies because we make wellies out of rubber.

The pupils should be able to identify the most important properties of any material used to create a particular object. For example, the function of an umbrella is to protect people from rain, therefore it must be made from a waterproof material that is also lightweight (so it can be carried), flexible (so it can be folded) and strong (so it can withstand heavy rain and wind).

Chocolate Teapots and Other Silly Objects

You could use the Michael Rosen poem "Woolly Saucepan" as a way to introduce this, or this video of an actual chocolate teapot being made https://www.dailymotion.com/video/x25oaff

Play a game of **That's Just Silly**. Ask them to think of different items, then list a silly material to make it from. Then think about the actual material and why that's used.

Object	Silly Material	Sensible Material	Why use the sensible material?
Wellington Boot	Newspaper	Rubber or plastic	Rubber and plastic are waterproof
Pillow	concrete	Foam	Foam is soft and flexible

Relate the discussion of materials to situations that the pupils will be familiar with. They will know that different clothes are suitable for different weather conditions. They should know that some materials are better for keeping them warm on a cold day and that some are more waterproof than others. They could look at objects such as their lunchboxes or pencil cases and think about what they are made from and why.

The story of the three little pigs can be a fun way of introducing the idea of the benefits of different building materials. Give the pupils a range of materials and ask them to build a house for the pigs.

Provide a range of resources for the pupils to use, such as: cocktail sticks, spaghetti, dominoes, sugar cubes, pipe cleaners, marshmallows, wine gums and drinking straws.

Give each group time to plan and build a house. Then use a hairdryer as the big bad wolf to see if each house can withstand a huff and a puff.

Types of rocks and the rock cycle

Rocks a vitally important to the world we live in. We use them in so many different ways. We use them in the construction of buildings, walls and roads, for sculpture and decoration and we even grind them up and put them in products such as toothpaste and makeup!

The KS2 unit on rocks follows on from the KS1 unit on properties of materials. It starts by looking at different types of rock and how they can be grouped by their simple properties. Start by taking the pupils on a walk around the school site to see how different rocks are being used.

What is a rock?

In everyday language, the word rock usually describes something big and heavy and is something different to a small stone or a pebble. But actually pebbles, stones and gravel are also rocks whether they are large or small.

Rock is a natural material, such as slate, marble or limestone. Not all natural, hard materials are rocks. Building materials such as brick and concrete can look a lot like rock but are not strictly rocks.

What is a Rock? https://www.bbc.co.uk/bitesize/topics/z9bbkqt/articles/zsgkdmn

Properties of Rocks

Rocks can be investigated using different properties, such as hardness, permeability, porosity and effect of acid. You can buy rock kits to do this with from most educational suppliers.

Hardness: rub different rocks against one another to see if they make a mark. This is a reflection of something called Moh's scale, which ranks rocks in order of how hard or soft they are.

Permeability: Drip water onto the rocks using a pipette. Does the water get soaked up by the rock or does it sit on the surface?

Porosity: Weigh the rocks dry, then immerse them in water for 5 minutes. Do they bubble? Remove the rocks, pat them dry and weigh them again. Which rocks have soaked up the most water?

Effect of Acid: Using a pipette and some strong vinegar, drip them onto the rock samples. Rocks that contain calcium carbonate, such as chalk, marble and limestone will fizz.

For more on how to do this, see page 10/11 of the pdf Rocks and Soils linked here https://edu.rsc.org/primary-science/rocks-and-soils-thats-chemistry/1795.article

Types of Rock

There are three broad categories of rock:

Igneous Rock: This is rock which is formed when molten lava or magma from inside the Earth cools and solidifies. This can happen when lava leaves a volcano in an eruption, but it can also happen below the surface, when magma gets close to the crust and cools. Igneous rocks often have crystals in them, formed as they cool. Igneous rocks include Granite and Basalt.

Sedimentary Rock: When rocks are eroded by wind and rain, they form a powder or sediment. This sediment ends up in lakes and rivers where it sinks to the bottom and becomes compressed. Sedimentary rock forms as layers of sediment (strata) compress the layers beneath them. Sedimentary rocks often contain fossils, as living things die and end up being buried by sediment. Examples of sedimentary rock include sandstone, limestone and chalk.

Metamorphic rock: These rocks are produced when igneous or metamorphic rocks experience intense heat or pressure. Metamorphic rocks form deep in the Earth's crust as the pressure of rock layers above them increases, along with the temperature. Examples of metamorphic rock include soapstone, marble and slate.

This website explains more: https://www.geolsoc.org.uk/ks3/gsl/education/resources/rockcycle/page3445.html

The Earth Science Education Unit has a virtual rock kit to explore different rocks https://www.earthscienceeducation.com/virtual_rock_kit/index.htm

Here's a fun activity to model the rock cycle and the formation of different types of rock using crayons https://youtu.be/WY5abXORFSk

How old are the rocks on Earth?

Some rocks on earth have been found to be very old indeed. A rock in Canada was found to contain minerals dating back over 4 billion years! This was one of the first rocks to form (on our planet) as our new planet began to cool.

But most rocks on Earth are a lot younger because natural processes are constantly breaking down existing rocks and creating new ones. We call this the rock cycle.

4.6 billion years ago the early Earth was a ball of molten rock which cooled and formed a solid crust. Molten rock, or magma, still exists below the surface. The crust is constantly moving, divided up into tectonic plates that can pull apart and push together or slide against each other. Plates can be pushed down deep into the Earth where the temperature is so hot it can melt rock back into magma

Volcanoes mostly occur along plate boundaries, where plates are pushed together or dragged apart. While people think of volcanoes as destructive things, they also have the power to create.

The molten rock coming out of a volcano is called lava. This lava flows away from the volcano and cools and hardens, forming new igneous rocks. In places with a lot of volcanoes like Hawaii and Iceland, new land is formed from molten lava.

In summary, while some rocks are very old, new rocks are being formed all the time from molten lava.

Fossils

A fossil is the preserved remains or traces of a dead organism. The process by which a fossil is formed is called fossilisation.

This page explains how fossils are made: https://www.nhm.ac.uk/discover/how-are-fossils-formed.html

Fossils tell us what animals and plants that lived millions of years ago looked like. We can tell a lot from fossils. Sometimes whole organisms fossilise, but you can learn a lot from smaller fossils such as teeth, leaves and even poo!

Mary Anning is an excellent example of a scientist to study when talking about fossils, either in year 3 or year 6. Much of our early information about fossils was down to her work. Some of the fossils she discovered are on display in the Natural History Museum in London.

The BBC produced an excellent video on her life here: https://youtu.be/qNOh-85_Dmc

It's commonly thought that the tongue twister "She sells seashells on the sea shore" is about Mary Anning!

What is Chalk?

Chalk forms giant features such as the iconic White Cliffs of Dover and is familiar to many of us as blackboard chalk. It is a soft, white porous sedimentary rock. Chalk is a more common name for a particular form of limestone called Cretaceous limestone.

Chalk is made up of the exoskeletons of millions of tiny sea creatures called plankton. When plankton dies the skeletons sink to the bottom of the ocean. Over time, these skeletons are compacted together to form rock. Chalk and other limestone contain many fossils since larger animals and plants can also sink to the bottom and be buried. Plants can also become fossilised and found in chalk.

Most of the chalk around today was formed between 144 to 66 million years ago. Chalk is white because it formed in very deep water so there were no other sediments to mix in with the plankton skeletons to add any other colours.

Soils

Soil is one of the world's most precious natural resources. It is vital for plant growth, providing food and materials for humans and animals; it regulates water by filtering out pollutants and can reduce flood risks; and it is home to a vast array of animals (OPAL).

When asked what soil is, pupils frequently suggested its main role was for growing plants (Space, 1993). Pupils might think of soil as something dull and brown, but soils come in a range of different types and differ from place to place. Some soils are very sandy, some can be orange or red or even dark black.

Soil itself is not a single substance but a combination of rocks, minerals, plant materials, animal materials, other microorganisms (which make organic matter), air and water. Plants then grow in these rock particles and when these (and animals) die, they decay and produce humus.

Decaying humus breaks down to release minerals for plants to utilise. Soils can have different properties, depending on the rocks that form them, and the organic matter created. Soil contains different layers of material, including topsoil, subsoil, weathered rocks and bedrock.

Study Different Soils

If you can get a range of soils, sandy, clay etc. the pupils can explore them in different ways.

Pupils could investigate different soils by exploring how they look, feel and smell. They could put samples in jam jars of water, shake them and let them settle. More ideas can be found here: https://www.gardenorganic.org.uk/sites/www.gardenorganic.org.uk/files/Sorting%20out%20Soils%20Activity%20Pack%20KS2.pdf

OPAL provide some excellent resources to carry out a soil and earthworm study in your local area, to look at the relationship between soil types and worms. Find out more here: https://www.imperial.ac.uk/opal/surveys/soilsurvey/

States of Matter and particle theory

What is everything made of? Everything that we can see, smell or touch is made from tiny particles called atoms. These can be arranged in different ways to make the solids, liquids and gases that make up your body and the world around you.

When asked to draw a solid, pupils will often draw something large and heavy. Objects such as a bag of rice or salt can be confusing since they don't behave exactly how a solid should – they can change their shape (Varelas et al, 2007). Similarly, a straw is not a solid because it is hollow.

Asking the pupils to categorise objects as solids, liquids and gases and including ambiguous materials such as this can help draw out these kinds of misconception and allow for discussion.

Solids, Liquids and Gases

In general, there are three states of matter. Solids, Liquids and Gases:

Solids: These are hard, and generally difficult to compress. They have a fixed shape.

Liquids: Liquids can flow and take the shape of the bottom of their container. They can't be squashed.

Gases: Gases are light and have no fixed shape or volume. They expand to fill whatever container they are put in.

Many objects are composite materials – they contain more than one type of material. Think of a football or a balloon, the skin is a solid, but it has a gas inside it. Toothpaste is a **colloid** – a mixture of thick liquid with small pieces of solid inside it. A foam, such as shaving foam or a sponge is a mixture of liquid with bubbles of gas throughout. Some liquids are emulsions (containing solid particles), for example blood, milk and paint.

The Particle Model

The particle model does not form part of the KS2 national curriculum, and it is a difficult concept for some, but teaching it in KS2 does make explaining Solids, liquids and gases in year 4 easier (Skamp, 2005). This also helps when talking about sound and vibrations later in year 4, when we need to talk about how vibrations travel in different materials. (See https://www.sciencefix.co.uk/2022/04/why-you-should-teach-about-particles-in-year-4/)

A solid is made of tightly bound particles. A solid is rigid and has a definite volume and shape. Think about a cup, it will still be cup-shaped wherever you put it. Because the particles are so close together, a solid cannot be compressed.

A liquid is a material made of vibrating particles which are very close together, but not as tightly bound as in a solid so they have more freedom to move. This means a liquid has a definite volume but no fixed shape. It can flow and take the shape of its container, but because the particles are close together a liquid cannot be compressed.

In gases the particles are not joined together and so are free to move and spread out. A gas has no fixed shape or volume and will expand to fill the entire space available to it.

You can explore the states of matter using this simulation from Phet: https://phet.colorado.edu/en/simulations/states-of-matter-basics

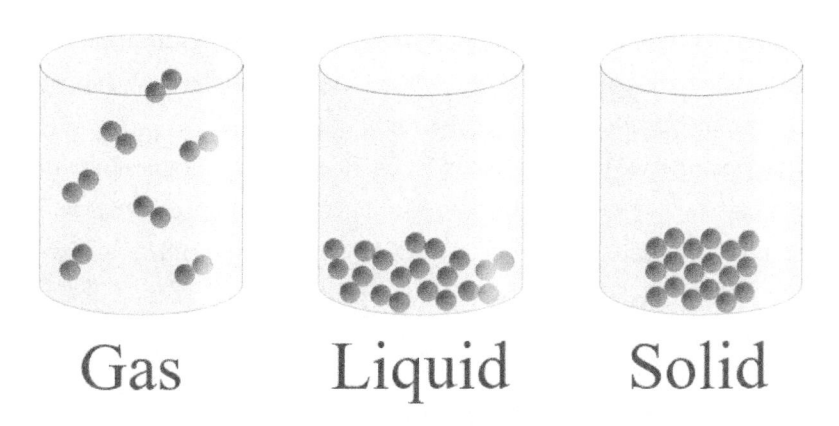

Gas   Liquid   Solid

https://commons.wikimedia.org/wiki/File:States_of_matter_En.svg

Use diagnostic questions to see what misconceptions the pupils have. Show them a deflated balloon then blow it up. Ask the pupils what they think will have happened to the mass of the balloon. Has the mass gone up, or down? Ask them to explain their reasoning. Some pupils will think that since gases are light, and that they float, the balloon will have become lighter.

Explain to the pupils that air is made of "stuff", or matter, made from particles. Air must have a mass, just like all materials. They probably would all agree that a balloon filled with water would have got heavier. Air also makes the balloon heavier, but by a very small amount. If we had some very accurate scales we could measure this difference and prove it.

Use a range of scenarios to discuss and objects for them to handle to make this as concrete as you can.

Changing State

What happens when an ice cube melts? Does it water it produces weigh the same as the original ice cube? What if you could capture all the water vapour as it evaporates, would that weigh the same too?

Ice, water and water vapour all consist of exactly the same water molecules, but in different states of matter. There's no chemical difference between these substances, just that the particles have arranged themselves differently.

If an ice cube melts into water, the total amount of particles will stay the same, and so the mass of ice will be the same as the water.

Most substances we know of can exist as solid, liquid, or gas. They may have very high or very low melting points, but eventually they can be changed. Iron can be turned into a liquid in a furnace. It is even possible to get solid oxygen or nitrogen if they are cooled enough. Oxygen freezes at -218°C and Nitrogen at -210°C!

Melting and Freezing

When heat energy is supplied to a solid, the particles vibrate more vigorously. Eventually, when given enough energy, they can break free from each other and move freely, becoming a liquid. This change is called melting.

Cooling a liquid down will cause the particles to move more slowly. If a liquid is cooled enough, its particles join back together to form a solid. We call this freezing.

Children will often just associate freezing with water turning into ice and cold temperatures, but the term applies to all liquids which become solids. Molten chocolate freezes to a solid around 35°C, whilst molten iron freezes around 1535°C.

Evaporating and Condensing

Heating a liquid makes its particles move more quickly. With enough energy, some particles near the surface overcome the forces of attraction and escape to become a gas. This is called evaporation.

If the temperature rises high enough, particles not just on the surface but anywhere in the liquid start to escape and form bubbles. At boiling point, the temperature remains the same, however strongly it's heated until all the liquid has become a gas. This takes place at a specific temperature for each pure liquid. In pure water this temperature is 100°C

Boiling is the change that takes place when a liquid is heated up to its boiling point.

Evaporation is the process where a liquid becomes a gas at temperatures below its boiling point.

Cooling a gas down to below its boiling point will cause particles to move more slowly. The gas changes back to a liquid; a change called condensing.

Exploring changes of state with pupils

Common misconceptions the pupils have include the idea that since gases can't be seen, there is nothing there and they have no mass. Or that water freezing or melting causes a change in mass. You can actively assess understanding in these areas, for instance by asking pupils to draw and annotate pictures and diagrams to demonstrate their understanding as they progress through the topic.

Tytler et al (2006) used a sequence of activities to model changes of state and relate them to particle diagrams. Pupils observe different activities and were encouraged to use the idea of particles in the diagrams they drew to explain what was happening. These included a cold can, to explain why condensation appears on the outside. A disappearing wet handprint and why the smell of eucalyptus oil spread through the class.

Allow them to observe phenomena for themselves, then ask them to explain what they see.

The Michael Rosen Poem "Chocolate" (http://www.stmp.camden.sch.uk/wp-content/uploads/2016/03/Wk-2-Rosen-1.pdf) is a great way to start the discussion on melting. Have the pupils hold a chocolate button on their hand for the duration of the poem! Is it still chocolate at the end?

The Water Cycle

Through the water cycle we can show that the Earth is a closed system. Water circulates in a constant cycle between the ocean, the atmosphere and the land. Water can be moved in many different forms, such as water vapour, rain, snow or hail. This BBC Bitesize Video explains more https://www.bbc.co.uk/bitesize/topics/zkgg87h/articles/z3wpp39

The Sun's energy warms liquid water in seas and lakes, making it **evaporate** into water vapour and rise into the atmosphere. Water within plants is also lost to the atmosphere in a process called transpiration. As this vapour rises, the air cools and the water vapour **condenses** into tiny water droplets, forming clouds.

Clouds are made from tiny droplets of water suspended in the air which are light enough to be held up by air currents. The water droplets in clouds eventually become so large that they fall as rain or snow (precipitation). The water will then eventually form rivers and flow to a lake or the sea where it starts the cycle again. Sometimes water can spend thousands of years locked up as snow or ice before melting and getting back to the sea.

This cycle has taken place for nearly 5 billion of years. Only a fraction of the water has been lost into space. So, in any glass of water there will be molecules of water that were drunk by dinosaurs, millions of years ago! See https://youtu.be/KK64DqpIy0s

Physical Changes

Physical changes can be changes of state – as explained in the last section or they can involve other processes such as dissolving. In a physical change, there is no new substance made and it can be easily reversed. This is different to a chemical change, where new substances are made, which we will look at in the next section.

Dissolving

Dissolving is an easy physical change to explore in the classroom. The liquids that allow dissolving are known as **solvents** and the solid that dissolved is known as the **solute**.

When a substance such as sugar dissolves, the granules of sugar break into small particles that are dispersed throughout the liquid until they are too small to see. The mixture of water and sugar particles is called a **solution**.

The dissolved sugar has not been chemically changed; sugar particles have not reacted with water particles. It is still sugar, with the same properties as before. Dissolving is a physical change.

You could demonstrate a model for dissolving to the pupils using a tray or shallow box with a layer of rice covering the bottom to represent particles of water. Add a handful of dried peas to represent the particles of sugar. Shake it up and eventually all the peas are mixed in amongst the water.

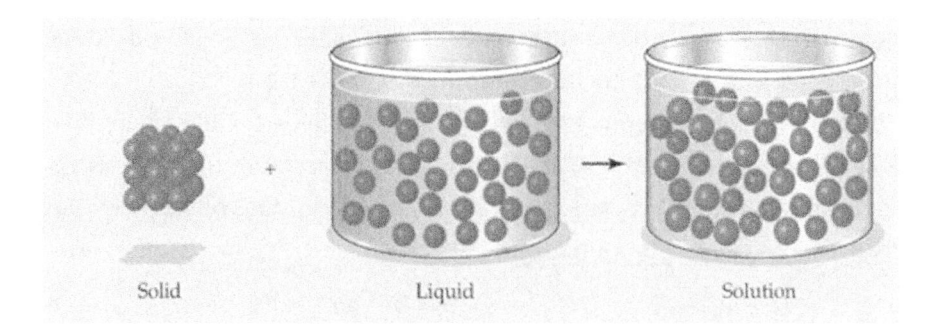

Solid   Liquid   Solution

Does it vanish?

Question: What happens if you dissolve 5g of sugar in 100g of water. How much does the solution weigh? 100g? 105g or something else? Pause and think before you read on.

When something like sugar is dissolved it doesn't vanish. Its particles have just mixed up with the particles of water. You can prove they are still there by tasting the liquid. You can still taste the sugar.

If you add 5g of sugar to 100g of water the overall weight of the solution is 105g. The sugar is still there. If you evaporate the water, the sugar is left behind.

On a related point, a can of diet coke will float in water, but regular coke will sink. Can you explain why?

Here's the answer: https://www.businessinsider.com/coke-diet-cola-floats-sinks-science-density-sugar-aspartame-2017-1?r=US&IR=T

Diet Coke and Mentos

This is a popular demonstration to do with the pupils as it gives a dramatic explosion of foam. But do be aware this is a physical change, not a chemical one.

The mints cause the dissolved carbon dioxide to be released from the soda, resulting in the massive release of foam. No new materials are formed.

This video explains more: https://www.eureka.org.uk/eureka-at-home/why-do-coke-and-mentos-have-such-a-messy-reaction/

Pupils could carry out an investigation into which drinks cause the highest plume. Is one brand of cola better than another? What about lemonade or sparkling water? Do cheaper supermarket brands work as well? What happens if you change the number of mints?

Tip: This works best if the cola is warm, so don't do it with bottles straight from the fridge! Diet Coke is better than regular coke as it's less sticky!

Separating Mixtures

A mixture forms when two or more materials are combined together but do not undergo a chemical change. Although the mixture may look different from its constituent parts, the original materials do not chemically change, and no new material is made.

Physical or mechanical processes can usually separate mixtures, although this is sometimes not always possible.

For more examples of separating mixtures, look here: **https://edu.rsc.org/primary-science/separating-mixtures-primary-science-video-demonstrations/912.article**

Chemical Changes

What happens when something goes rusty? Or when you cook your dinner? What kind of reactions are taking place? Chemical changes are all around us, and many are easy to explore in the classroom.

A chemical change is a process in which two or more substances react together to produce a new substance. The chemicals might join together in new ways, or break apart and re-join, forming new chemical substances.

Chemical changes cannot be easily reversed. They are known as irreversible reactions.

Examples of chemical reactions include cooking, burning and rusting. Cooking foods generally change their chemical structure irreversibly, and the resultant foods often have different properties to the original.

Burning is a chemical reaction. When something like paper burns, new chemicals are produced – such as carbon dioxide and water vapour. Ash (carbon) is also produced.

Think about how an egg changes when heated. How is a fried egg different to a raw egg? Could you change a fried egg back to a raw egg?

Signs of a chemical reaction

There are often noticeable signs that a chemical reaction is taking place. There might be a flame, or bubbles of gas produced. It might change colour or give off light (as in glowsticks).

The reacting chemicals might get hot and give off heat. These are known as exothermic reactions. Some reactions get colder. They absorb heat and are called endothermic reactions.

Chemical Changes in the Classroom

A challenge in teaching this topic is finding good practical opportunities that are safe to do in the primary classroom, and which do not require complicated equipment.

As with all practical work, refer to safety guides and carry out a risk assessment. It's always a good idea to test these out yourself before you use them with a class.

The Royal Society of Chemistry has some good practical ideas and demonstrations you can try: https://edu.rsc.org/primary-science/changing-materials-primary-science-video-demonstrations/913.article

Fizz Bang Rockets can be an interesting investigation if you change the number of tablets or amount of water. This guide from Alka Seltzer explains more https://www.alkaseltzer.com/original/science-experiments/rockets

Making a bicarbonate volcano is also common way to demonstrate a chemical change. This guide from the Natural History Museum explains how to do it https://www.nhm.ac.uk/discover/how-to-make-a-volcano.html

Elephant Toothpaste is another fun demo. There are different recipes out there, some safer than others. The safest one for schools involves hydrogen peroxide and yeast. Here's a good guide from Steve Spangler Science https://www.stevespanglerscience.com/lab/experiments/elephants-toothpaste/

Make clear the differences between chemical and physical changes. A chemical change is a reaction where new substances are produced. It is not easily reversible. A physical change is a reaction where no new substances are produced. They are usually reversible.

Mixtures and Compounds

Some children find it difficult to understand the difference between the terms mixture and compound. They have very specific meanings in science.

A **mixture** forms when two or more materials are combined together but do not undergo a chemical change. Although the mixture may be very different from its constituent parts, the original materials do not chemically change, and no new material is made.

Physical or mechanical processes can usually separate mixtures, although this is not always possible – for example when one substance forms a coating around another. Mixtures can take the form of solids, liquids or gases or they can even be a combination of all three.

An **element** is the simplest form of a chemical substance, containing a single type of atom. Examples of elements include gold, copper, oxygen and hydrogen.

A **compound** is made from several elements that join together in a reaction. Water is a compound formed from the reaction between hydrogen gas and oxygen gas. One molecule of water is made from two hydrogen atoms joined to one oxygen (H_2O). Other compounds, such as plastics, or the proteins in our bodies, can be made up of long chains of hundreds of atoms.

Many of the materials we encounter each day are compounds. Many compounds can be put into mixtures without reacting further. For example, salt and water are both compounds, but they can be mixed together to form salty water, which is a mixture.

Useful Links

Allen, M., (2016). The Best Ways to Teach Primary Science. Open University Press. Chapter5 Properties of Everyday Materials

BBC. Mary Anning Video: https://youtu.be/qNOh-85_Dmc

BBC Bitesize: What is soil? https://school-learningzone.co.uk/key_stage_two/ks2_science/materials/rocks_and_soil/rocks_and_soil.html

BBC bitesize What is a rock? https://www.bbc.co.uk/bitesize/topics/z9bbkqt/articles/zsgkdmn

BBC Bitesize: What is the Water Cycle https://www.bbc.co.uk/bitesize/topics/zkgg87h/articles/z3wpp39

Curious Minds. (2015) Have you drunk Dinosaur Pee? https://youtu.be/KK64DqpIy0s

Earth Science Education Unit: https://www.earthscienceeducation.com/resources/index.htm

Geological Society, The Rock Cycle https://www.geolsoc.org.uk/ks3/gsl/education/resources/rockcycle/page3445.html

Hamilton Trust / STEM Learning: Everyday Materials: Let's Build https://w

ww.stem.org.uk/rxuat

Natural History Museum. How are Dinosaur Fossils Made? https://www.nhm.ac.uk/discover/how-are-fossils-formed.html

Nicholson, D. (2019) Rainbow Skittles Experiment for Kids https://www.sciencefix.co.uk/2020/10/rainbow-skittles-experiment-for-kids/

Nicholson, D. (2019) Make a Lava Lamp in a Bottle https://www.sciencefix.co.uk/2019/10/make-a-lava-lamp-in-a-bottle/

Nicholson, D. (2019) How to turn milk into plastic https://www.sciencefix.co.uk/2019/07/how-to-turn-milk-into-plastic-just-add-vinegar/

Nicholson, D. (2019) Sand Table Science Ideas: https://www.sciencefix.co.uk/2019/04/early-years-sand-table-science-ideas/

Nicholson, D. (2019) Water Table Science Ideas: https://www.sciencefix.co.uk/2019/04/early-years-water-table-science-ideas/

Nicholson, D. (2022) Why You Should Teach About Particles in Year 4. https://www.sciencefix.co.uk/2022/04/why-you-should-teach-about-particles-in-year-4/

Rosen, M., (2000) Centrally Heated Knickers. Puffin Books.

Royal Society of Chemistry. Rocks and Soils: https://edu.rsc.org/primary-science/rocks-and-soils-thats-chemistry/1795.article

Royal Society of Chemistry. The Properties of Materials And Their Everyday Uses https://edu.rsc.org/primary-science/the-properties-of-materials-and-their-everyday-uses-thats-chemistry/1792.article?adredir=1

Royal Society of Chemistry: Grouping and Classifying Materials Using Their Properties https://edu.rsc.org/primary-science/grouping-and-classifying-materials-thats-chemistry/1791.article

OPAL Soil and Earthworm Study https://www.imperial.ac.uk/opal/surveys/soilsurvey/

Skamp, K., (2005) Teaching About Stuff. Primary Science Review 89: 20-22. https://www.dropbox.com/s/tup07n3g3yk0v31/PSR%20Sep%2005%20Talking%20about%20stuff.pdf?dl=0

SPACE Project Research Report (1993) Rocks, Soil and Weather. https://www.stem.org.uk/resources/elibrary/resource/29211/space-project-research-report-rocks-soil-and-weather

Varelas, M., Pappas, C.C., Kane, J.M., Arsenault, A., Hankes, J. and Cowan, B.M. (2008), Urban primary-grade pupils think and talk science: Curricular and instructional practices that nurture participation and argumentation. Sci. Ed., 92: 65-95. https://doi.org/10.1002/sce.20232

Natural History Museum. How to make a volcano https://www.nhm.ac.uk/discover/how-to-make-a-volcano.html

Rosen, M., (2000) Centrally Heated Knickers. Puffin Books.

Royal Society of Chemistry. The Life of Water https://edu.rsc.org/resources/the-life-of-water/1651.article

Royal Society of Chemistry Separating Mixtures: https://edu.rsc.org/primary-science/separating-mixtures-primary-science-video-demonstrations/912.article

Royal Society of Chemistry: Changing Materials https://edu.rsc.org/primary-science/changing-materials-primary-science-video-demonstrations/913.article

Royal Society of Chemistry: Separating Sand and Sawdust https://edu.rsc.org/resources/separating-sand-sawdust-and-salt/1189.article

Spangler, S: Elephants Toothpaste https://www.stevespanglerscience.com/lab/experiments/elephants-toothpaste/

Tytler, R. & Peterson, S. & Prain, Vaughan. (2006). Picturing evaporation: Learning science literacy through a particle representation. Teaching Science. 52. 12-17. https://blogs.deakin.edu.au/asell-for-schools-vic/wp-content/uploads/sites/160/2018/03/Tytler-et-al-Teach_Sci_evap.pdf

7

Forces

What are forces?

We can't see them, but forces are a vital part of our lives. Without an understanding of forces, our houses would collapse and our cars would crash. So, what are forces, and what do pupils need to know about them?

In Early Years, pupils experience a range of toys and play equipment that can be moved by pushing or pulling. Across the EYFS areas of learning this can include using puppets, reading pop-up books, performing action rhymes, threading beads, digging and lifting sand, riding bikes, weaving and playing percussion instruments (Thornton and Brunton, 2006). Go on a push and pull walk to see examples of things being pushed and pulled (Page, 2011).

At Key Stage 1, while there is no longer a standalone Pushes and Pulls unit, pupils are introduced to the idea of pushes and pulls within the Year 2 Uses of Everyday Materials unit in the context of changing shape of a material such as modelling clay.

"Find out how the shapes of solid objects made from some materials can be changed by squashing, bending, twisting and stretching." (NC 2014)

What words can they use to describe what they do to the clay (squeeze, twist, bend, squash, flatten etc). Make a model out of the clay, when are they pushing the clay and when are they pulling it?

A force is always a push, a pull or a twist (push one side, pull the other) as explained here https://www.bbc.co.uk/bitesize/topics/zn77hyc/articles/zptckqt

In Year 3, the Forces unit is mainly concerned with comparing how things move on different surfaces (and also Magnets, which we'll look at later). Year 5 is the main unit where the pupils explore forces and their effects.

Forces are measured in **Newtons** (N) and can be measured using a Force Meter / Newton meter. This video explains how to use one https://youtu.be/SWOmsKkP8ZY

May the Force Be With You

It might help by thinking of all the different, non-science, uses of the word "Force" that we use. May the Force Be With You is one example, but also things like Armed Forces, Police Force, A force for good etc.

Can you think of any others?

You could brainstorm this with a class as a starter activity. For most of us the word Force often implies "getting something done" or making something do something. You can then introduce what scientists mean by the word "Force" which is a push or a pull. A force can cause an object to speed up, slow down or change shape.

Static Objects and Balanced Forces

If an object is stationary, then all the forces on it must be balanced. So, a book sitting on a table is pushing down with a force of, let's say 5N. What pupils find hard to understand is that if the book is not moving, then the table is also pushing upwards on the book with an identical force of 5N. This is called a **reactive force**.

If these forces were not balanced, then the book would either fall through the table, or be pushed up into the air.

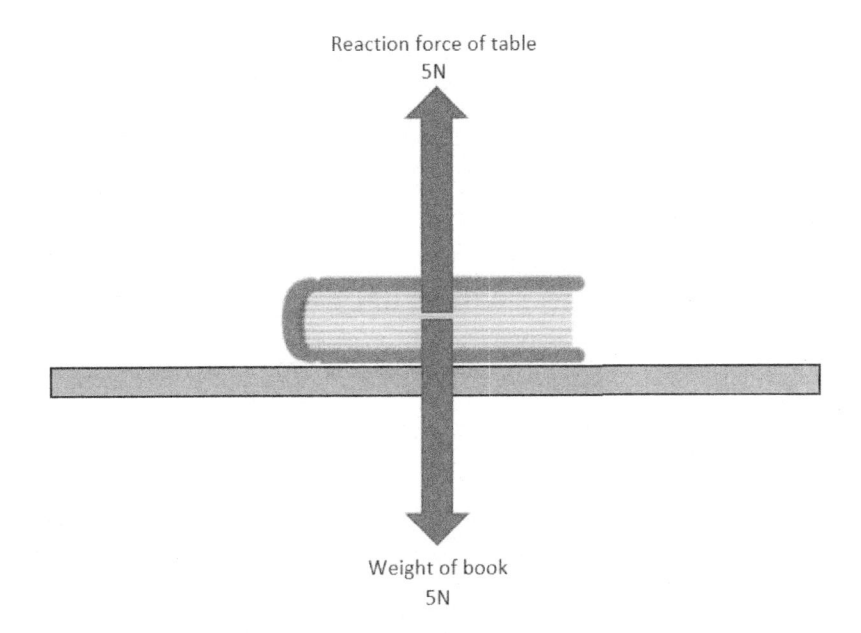

Reaction force of table 5N (upward arrow)

Weight of book 5N (downward arrow)

"Seeing" the Forces

Ask the pupils to imagine they can see the forces at work. Perhaps putting on a special pair of glasses to "see" the forces (cheap plastic sunglasses or 3D glasses from a cinema). Show the pupils simple situations like a toy hanging on a piece of string, a helium balloon, a toy duck floating in a bowl of water, a book on a cushion etc.

Perrin (2012) suggests the pupils answer three questions when observing:

- Where is the force acting?
- What is providing the force?
- What kind of force is it?

Use words like gravity, upthrust, pull, push, resistance, friction etc. Give the pupils cardboard arrows or post-it notes to label the forces at work.

These resources from the IOP can help with misconceptions: https://spark.iop.org/many-pupils-have-difficulty-using-arrows-indicate-direction-and-point-action-force

Mass and Weight

In everyday language, we use the words Mass and Weight to mean the same thing, but for a scientist, they mean slightly different things.

Your mass is how much of you there is, and your weight is the force you exert on the floor because of gravity.

Mass is the amount of material or "matter" in an object, measured in kilograms (kg). The mass of an astronaut would be the same on Earth as it would be in space. They haven't gained or lost any mass going into space.

Weight is a force that changes in relation to the force of gravity. On Earth, gravity causes objects to accelerate towards its centre with a force of approximately 10N for every kilogram. An astronaut with a mass of 60kg has a weight of 600N on Earth. On the moon, the pull of gravity is much less, about 1/6 that on Earth. A 60kg astronaut would only weigh 100N on the moon.

Try this out: Explore balancing forces using this simulator from Phet: https://phet.colorado.edu/en/simulations/forces-and-motion-basics How could you use this in a classroom?

Moving objects

Forces can make an object speed up, slow down, change shape and change direction. On Earth, for something to keep moving, such as a car or a plane, a force needs to be applied otherwise air resistance and friction will slow it down and bring it to a stop. When something like a car is travelling at a steady speed, all the forces acting upon it are balanced.

Balanced Forces

A common misconception is that forces always act in pairs that are equal and opposite. The misconception comes from Newton's third law of motion; "For every action there is an equal and opposite reaction". But if this was true then nothing would ever move because the forces would always be perfectly balanced.

While it is true that forces do usually act in pairs, it does not automatically mean they are equal. Forces are only balanced if the object is moving at a steady speed or not moving at all. Imagine a "tug of war" and each side is pulling with the same force, then the forces are balanced, and the rope will not move. If one side pulls with more force the rope will move towards them.

When a car starts moving, the force pushing it forward is greater than the friction/air resistance trying to slow it down so it starts to accelerate. When it is travelling at a steady speed along the road, the forward force is equal to the air resistance/friction. These forces are now balanced.

If the driver applies the brakes, the forces are unbalanced again; the resistance/friction is now higher than the force moving the car forwards and so the car slows down and will eventually stop.

Gravity

The force that pulls things to the centre of the Earth (and other planets) is called gravity. The larger and heavier the object, the greater the pull of gravity it has. An object as massive as the Sun has a strong enough pull of gravity to keep all the planets in the solar system in orbit around it, even as far out as Pluto and beyond!

What is Gravity: https://www.bbc.co.uk/bitesize/topics/zf66fg8/articles/zqbm3k7

Gravity is different on other planets. Some planets, like Jupiter, have a much higher pull of gravity than Earth. Some planets, like Mercury, have a much lower pull of gravity. This activity from The Ogden Trust allows pupils to experience what that might feel like. How would it feel to lift the same object on different planets? https://www.ogdentrust.com/resources/phizzi-practical-planetary-picnic

Balloon Rockets

A fun way to investigate moving is to inflate a balloon and let it go. The air rushes out the end of the balloon in one direction, creating a force that propels the balloon in the other direction. Attach the balloon to some thread running across the room using a drinking straw to keep the rocket flying straight. More details here https://spark.iop.org/collections/marvin-and-milo#balloon-rocket

A balloon attached to a drinking straw can be used as a "rocket engine" for rocket cars designed by the pupils. They could use a plastic bottle or chip tray as the chassis and bottle tops as wheels. The Bloodhound Supersonic Car project produced this guide you can use. https://www.stem.org.uk/elibrary/resource/26239

Air resistance and friction

If an astronaut in space threw a ball then it would keep moving forever. It would keep going in a straight line and it would only stop (or change direction) if it hit another object or got caught up in the gravity of something big like a star or a planet. This would apply another force to the ball which would change how it moves.

This doesn't happen if we were to throw a ball on Earth. The ball would eventually come to a stop because of forces such as friction, gravity and air resistance. These forces act on any moving object and eventually bring it to a stop.

Newton's first law of motion states that an object will continue at a constant speed and in the same direction unless a force acts upon it. This means that even if an object is travelling at high speed, no force is required to maintain the speed. A force is only required if the object is to change the speed at which it is moving. Hence, a force is required for acceleration, deceleration or a change of direction.

Friction

Friction is the force created between two surfaces when they rub together. Rough surfaces create more friction than smooth surfaces.

Friction can be useful. We need a high grip between the soles of our shoes and the ground, or between our car tyres and the road. Brakes rely on friction to slow a car or bike down. A parachute increases the air resistance and slows the parachutist down so that they can land safely.

Other times, friction can be something we want to reduce; we will add oil or lubricant to door hinges and the hubs of our bicycles to reduce friction and make them move more easily.

What is friction? https://www.bbc.co.uk/bitesize/topics/zsxxsbk/articles/zxqrdxs

Introduce friction as something that produces heat and allow pupils to feel the frictional forces by rubbing their hands together (Burton, 2012). Then rub them gently over different grades of sandpaper.

Pupils can use a force meter and drag a shoe across the floor to see what force is needed to pull it along. They could then pull the same shoe across different surfaces, such as a tabletop, playground and grass to observe how friction changes. They could also investigate different shoes, keeping the surface the same, to see which shoes have the most grip (highest friction). (See https://www.ogdentrust.com/resources/phizzi-enquiry-slippy-shoes)

Air Resistance

Air resistance is the force that acts between a moving object and the air molecules around it, slowing the object down.

To see the effect of air resistance, drop a sheet of paper and watch how it falls. Then crumple it into a ball and drop it again. The mass of the paper hasn't changed, but the ball of paper falls much faster because it is in contact with less air as it falls, so it experiences less air resistance.

Modern cars and planes are designed to be streamlined, to reduce air resistance and move faster.

If you remove the air, there is no air resistance. A bowling ball and a feather will fall at exactly the same rate. Watch this video with Brian Cox to find out more: https://youtu.be/E43-CfukEgs

Investigating Air Resistance

A classic investigation into air resistance is to use paper helicopters or parachutes. There are lots of variables pupils can change and

Helicopters – change the size or the shape of the wings to see the effect on the time it takes to fall. Could also change the overall size or material the helicopters are made from. This resource explains more https://www.stem.org.uk/resources/elibrary/resource/34163/paper-helicopters-science

Parachutes – change the size of the parachute or the material that it is made from. See what effect it has on the time to fall. This video explains more; https://www.bbc.co.uk/teach/class-clips-video/science-design-and-technology-ks2-harnessing-air-resistance-with-parachutes/zjps382

Simple machines - gears, levers, pulleys

The invention of levers, wheels, gears and pulleys transformed the way we lived. It allowed our ancestors to build bigger and more complex places to live and work, allowed us to irrigate fields, grind flour, transport heavy loads, travel to distant places and much more. But how do they work?

The three simple machines outlined by the National Curriculum are levers, pulleys and gears. Let's look at each of these.

Levers

Levers can be demonstrated by using a meter rule or metal rod to lift a heavy object. A simple demonstration is showing how to push a door open. If you push close to the hinge it is very hard to move the door, if you push near where the handle is it should be very easy. The door is acting as a lever, you have to move a lot more, but you can use a much lower force.

Super Simple Machines: Levers https://youtu.be/lueqEolxLyc

Explore making a see saw balance with this simulation from Phet https://phet.colorado.edu/en/simulations/balancing-act

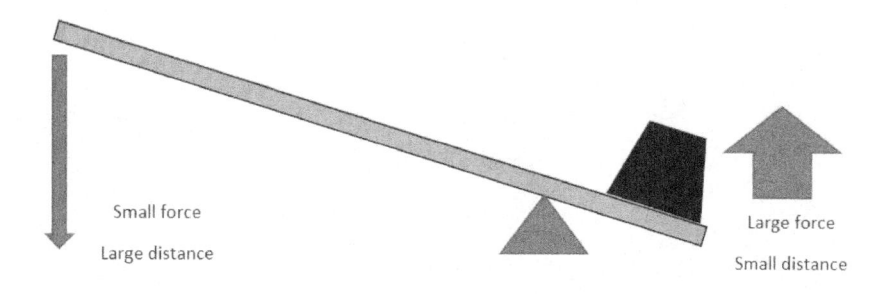

Small force, Large distance — Large force, Small distance

Gears

Gears are wheels with teeth that interlock together. Turning one gear makes the other one turn. If the gears are different sizes they can be used to increase the power of a turning force. Turning a small wheel slowly will move the larger wheel slower but with more force.

You can explore gears with simple toys with interlocking gears. You could even bring in a bike to look at how its gears work.

What is a gear? https://youtu.be/cShBlYP6uuo

Pulleys

Like a lever, pulleys trade force for distance. Using several pulleys, you would need to pull a rope over a longer distance, but with a much lower force – allowing you to lift a heavy object easily. This guide explains more: https://science.howstuffworks.com/transport/engines-equipment/pulley.htm

Pulleys can be bought from educational suppliers or can be built out of cotton reels and suchlike.

Watch this video for more: https://youtu.be/Nj4J7QNeBNk

Heath Robinson Machines

Pupils could be shown various Heath Robinson or Rube Goldberg machines which use over-elaborate engineering to carry out different tasks. They might already be familiar with some of the inventions of Wallace and Gromit.

They could design some crazy inventions of their own that use pulleys, gears and levers. They might also be able to build some in the classroom.

For a cool, real-life example of a Heath Robinson machine, show the pupils this music video from OK Go: https://youtu.be/qybUFnY7Y8w

Exploring Forces

There are lots of different STEM challenges that the pupils can take part in to explore forces with real world applications and problem-solving opportunities. Challenge the pupils to build the tallest tower out of spaghetti or protect an egg from falling.

The Rochester Bridge Trust produce some excellent resources about bridges and how to build different types of bridge. You can access them here: https://rochesterbridgetrust.org.uk/learning-activities/learning-about-bridges/. Also check out the book Mr Shaha's Marvellous Machines for ideas of things they can build from everyday items.

Magnets

Magnets were known about by Ancient Greeks and Early Chinese as early as 500BC. Special rocks called Lodestones were used for navigation. These were hung from a string and pointed south. The name magnet comes from a region of Greece called Magnesia, where lodestones were found.

In Early Years and KS1 – pupils can explore using magnets. See what things stick to a magnet, and what things don't. They could sort materials into two groups, based on whether they are magnetic or not.

Young pupils do not generally know about what materials a magnet will stick to, often including metals such as gold and aluminium, but also non-metals such as wood, cloth and glass (Christidou et al. 2009). Pupils might have seen cartoons and movies where a super magnet attracts every single metal object nearby (Postman Pat and Paw Patrol both have an episode where this happens!) which doesn't help with this misconception.

Magnetic materials are always made of metal. But not all metals are magnetic. Iron, nickel and cobalt are magnetic. Steel is magnetic because it contains iron (but some types of stainless steel are not magnetic.) See: https://www.bbc.co.uk/bitesize/topics/zyttyrd/articles/zw889qt

The year 3 Forces and Magnets unit is where most of the work on magnets will take place. Magnetic forces can act at a distance, without direct contact, like gravity. Stick a magnet on top of a small toy car and push it with another magnet – it's possible to make the car move without having to touch it.

Magnets have two poles, called North and South. If you hold two magnets close together with opposite poles pointing towards each other they will attract and stick together. If you hold the magnets with the same poles together, North against North or South against South, then the magnets will push each other away, or repel.

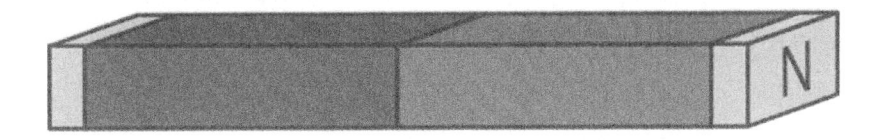

A magnetic compass works because planet Earth has its own magnetic field. It acts as if there is a giant bar magnet inside it. What we call the North pole of a magnet is technically the North-seeking pole. If you hang a magnet on a piece of string and allow it to move freely, the N pole is attracted to the North pole of the Earth. (Which, stay with me here, must be a magnetic south pole, as it attracts the N pole...). Likewise, the South pole of the magnet is the south-seeking pole, pointing to the South pole of the planet. You can read more about this here: https://www.explainthatstuff.com/how-compasses-work.html

Making a Magnet

It is possible to turn a steel paperclip into a magnet. First straighten it out and then use a regular magnet and stroke the paperclip repeatedly in one direction only. After 10 strokes, see if it will pick up another paperclip. If not, stroke another 10 times and repeat.

This works because the atoms inside a piece of metal act like tiny mini-magnets called domains. Usually, they are all pulling in all different directions and cancelling out each other's effects, so the material is not magnetic.

https://www.electronics-tutorials.ws/electromagnetism/magnetism.html

If you stroke a metal such as iron, steel or cobalt with another magnet the domains can all line up and point in the same direction. This reinforces their overall effect, and the metal becomes magnetic. In non-magnetic metals the domains cannot move, and so the metal cannot become magnetic.

Over time, they'll move back out of line and lose their magnetism again. This is also why dropping and mistreating school magnets eventually makes them become weaker and lose their magnetism. So, treat them nicely!

Useful Links

Allen, M., (2016) The Best Ways to Teach Primary Science. Research into Practice. OUP. Ch 11. Forces and Magnets.

BBC Class Clips : Harnessing Air Resistance with Parachutes: https://www.bbc.co.uk/teach/class-clips-video/science-design-and-technology-ks2-harnessing-air-resistance-with-parachutes/zjps382

Brian Cox Visits World's Biggest Vacuum https://youtu.be/E43-CfukEgs

Burton, B. (2012) Experiencing Friction in First Grade. *Science and Pupils*, v50 n2 p68-72 Oct 2012 https://eric.ed.gov/?id=EJ1001646

Cool Science Experiments: Make a Floating Needle Compass https://www.electronics-tutorials.ws/electromagnetism/magnetism.html

Compound Chemistry: The Metals in UK Coins https://www.compoundchem.com/2014/03/27/the-metals-in-uk-coins/

Keeley, P., (2011) Formative Assessment Probes: Pushes and Pulls Science and Pupils, v49 n2 p28-30. https://eric.ed.gov/?id=EJ944183

How Stuff Works: Pulleys https://science.howstuffworks.com/transport/engines-equipment/pulley.htm

National Curriculum for Science (2014) https://assets.publishing.service.gov.uk/government/uploads/system/uploads/attachment_data/file/425618/PRIMARY_national_curriculum_-_Science.pdf

Perrin, G. (2012) Wearing Forces Spectacles Primary Science 124 pp32-33 https://www.ase.org.uk/resources/primary-science/issue-124/wearing-forces-spectacles

Rochester Bridge Trust: Learning About Bridges https://rochesterbridgetrust.org.uk/learning-activities/learning-about-bridges/

Shaha, A., and Robertson, E., (2021) Mr Shaha's Marvellous Machines. Scribble

STEM Learning – Paper Helicopters https://www.stem.org.uk/resources/elibrary/resource/34163/paper-helicopters-science

The Early Years Handbook (2004) Support for practitioners in the Foundation Stage edited by Max de Boo

Thornton, L., and Brunton., P. (2006) Early Years Science: Forces. Nursery World. https://www.nurseryworld.co.uk/features/article/early-years-science-forces

8

The Earth in Space

Movement of the Earth, Sun and Moon

Humans have been fascinated with space for thousands of years. Many of our early civilizations, such as the Ancient Egyptians, Chinese, Mayans and Babylonians studied the stars and the moon. This whole topic area can really capture the awe and wonder of science but can be very daunting.

The Earth is one of 8 planets that travels around the Sun in a solar system. This is the **heliocentric** model (sun at the centre) first proposed by Copernicus in 1543.

It takes the Earth 365 and a quarter days to make one complete orbit of the Sun. We call this a year. We add up the extra quarter days, and every 4 years add a whole day to the calendar. This is why we get leap years.

A moon is an object that orbits a planet. Our planet has just one moon, but other planets have many more. Our moon orbits the Earth once every 28 days. We call this a month (from moonth!)

The Ogden Trust has a resource that covers how our ideas about the motion of the Sun and Earth have changed over time. https://www.ogdentrust.com/resources/research-cards-earth-and-space

How do we get day and night?

A common misconception pupils have is the idea that Earth is fixed and the Sun moves around us (Osbourne et al, 1994). It's easy to come to that conclusion since from our point of view we appear stationary, and the Sun seems to move across the sky. At dawn, the Sun rises in the east, becoming high in the sky by the middle of the day, and then at dusk, it sets in the west.

In reality, it is not the Sun that's moving but our planet, Earth, as it orbits around the Sun. Over the course of a day, the Earth spins, or rotates, anticlockwise around an invisible line called the axis. The axis runs from the North Pole to the South Pole.

Night and Day

It takes 24 hours for the Earth to make one complete rotation on its axis. We call this a day. At any time, half the earth is facing the sun and is lit up by sunlight. We call this day. At the same time, half the Earth is facing away from the Sun, receiving no sunlight at all. We call this night.

This video explains more: https://www.bbc.co.uk/bitesize/clips/z9fpyrd

Pupils will probably have friends or relatives in other countries and will know that some countries have their night time when we have our daytime. They might know that some countries are ahead of us in time, whilst others are behind in time. They might be having dinner when we're having breakfast. Use the internet to look at webcams from countries where it might be the middle of the night

Models of Sun, Earth and Moon

It would be useful to have a selection of different-sized balls, which can be used to model the Earth, Moon and Sun. Inflatable globes are more easily stored than regular globes. Use a torch to play the role of the Sun; shine them onto a globe or ball to demonstrate night and day.

You could make a model of the Earth, Sun and Moon using paper discs,

sheets of card and paper fasteners as outlined here: https://www.science
fix.co.uk/2019/07/quick-science-idea-sun-earth-and-moon-papercraft-
model/

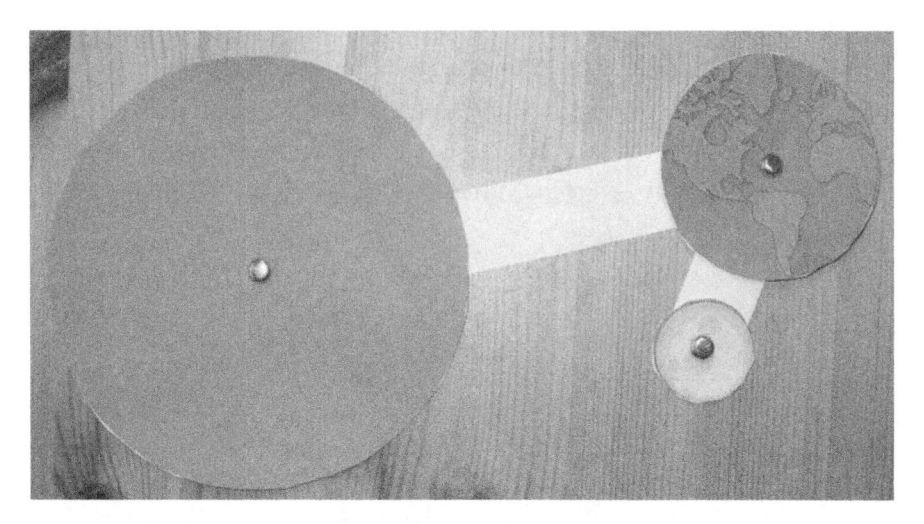

For a physical demonstration, the pupils could model the motion of the sun, earth and moon on the playground or field. Have several pupils holding hands in a circle to act as the sun. Three pupils could then hold hands to act as the Earth. They can start moving in a circle around the sun, while also spinning around. One child could also be the moon, running in a circle around the Earth as it goes around the Sun.

On a sunny day, pupils stand on the playground and draw around their shadows in the morning. Then stand in the same spot and repeat at different times during the day. They should be able to see the direction of their shadow changing.

This article by Tom Sherrington, is a good discussion of some of the teaching and learning involved in a concept such as "why does the sun rise in the east". https://teacherhead.com/2021/06/06/my-favourite-cpd-question-for-weaving-teaching-concepts-and-strategies-together/

THE EARTH IN SPACE

How do the seasons change?

In KS1, pupils should understand that there are different seasons, but they do not need to explain why. As a class, observe the seasons with the pupils over the school year. Pick an area of the school which has trees and plants and take photographs of how they look. Record the temperature, and any other weather observations they can make. They could also make a note of the time of sunset and sunrise throughout the year.

Repeat this every week or every month to build up a bank of images and observations. There could even be a display board in the classroom devoted to displaying some of their photographs so far and their weather observations. There are lots of opportunities here for lots of art activities based around the various seasons throughout the year.

Pupils should see that there are marked changes over the course of a year. They should be able to say what the changes are in each season. If you can, try and make contact with a school in the Southern Hemisphere to see what the seasonal changes are like for them. They could find out why Australians like to have Christmas on the beach!

Planning to teach Seasonal Changes

Whilst it is possible to teach this as a single block of lessons, this topic is best set up in September and run as an ongoing project through the year. Weather monitoring and observing plants can then be run once a week or once a month to build up a bank of observations.

This data can then be presented and discussed towards the end of the school year. Do remember to save any images and weather data centrally so it could be used by other classes the following year and added to.

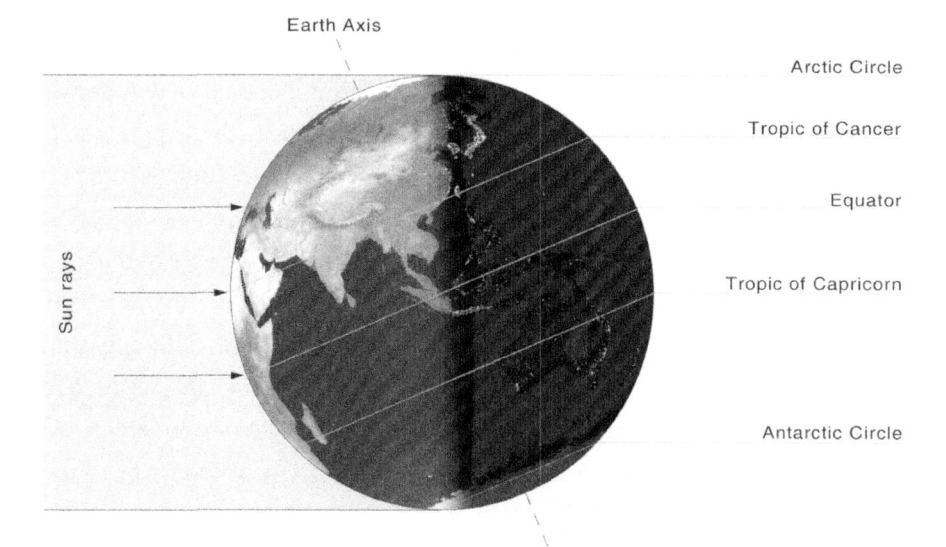

Earth Axis — *Arctic Circle* — *Tropic of Cancer* — *Equator* — *Tropic of Capricorn* — *Antarctic Circle* — *Sun rays*

https://commons.wikimedia.org/wiki/File:Earth-lighting-summer-solstice_CAT.png#/media/File:Earth-lighting-summer-solstice_EN.png

Why do we get Seasons?

After introducing the idea of seasons in KS1, pupils won't have to try and explain why we get seasons until upper Key Stage 2. It can be quite a difficult concept to understand.

The Earth's axis is tilted at an angle of 23.5°. It is this tilt that gives us the seasons.

The common misconception is that we are closer to the Sun in summer which makes us hotter (Osbourne et al. 1994), but this isn't true. We're actually closest in spring and autumn. The tilt changes the angle at which sunlight hits us.

In Winter, the northern hemisphere tilts away from the Sun. The sunlight that reaches the northern hemisphere is weaker and colder because it is spread over a bigger area. This gives us the cold temperatures associated with winter.

In Summer, the northern hemisphere tilts towards the Sun, while the

THE EARTH IN SPACE

southern hemisphere tilts towards it. The sunlight that reaches the northern hemisphere is stronger and hotter because it is concentrated in a small area. This gives us the hotter, summer temperatures.

The southern hemisphere points the other way, so when it is summer in the northern hemisphere, it's winter in the southern hemisphere. Countries on the Equator stay roughly at the same angle towards the sun over the year, so they stay pretty constant all year round.

This video explains more: https://youtu.be/WgHmqv__-UbQ

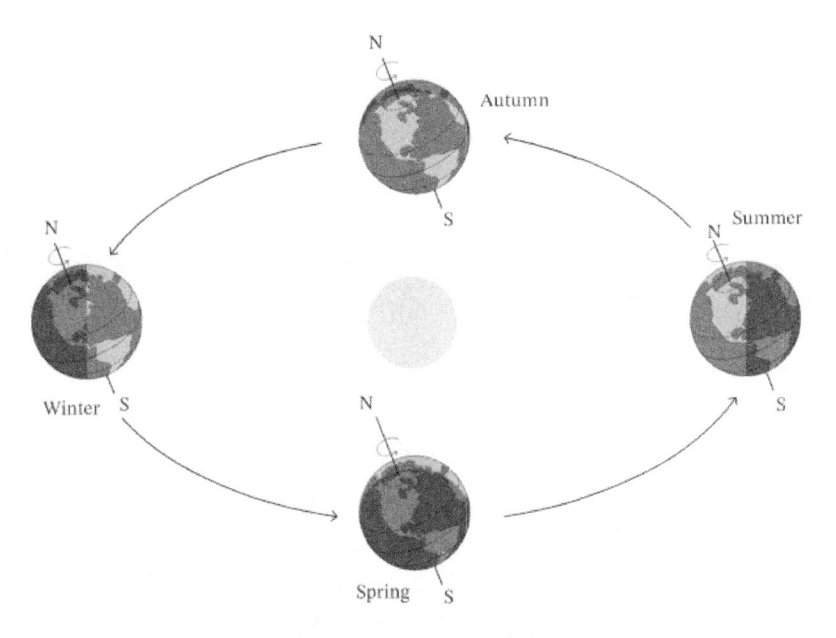

https://commons.wikimedia.org/wiki/File:Orbital_relations_of_the_Solstice,_Equinox_%26_Intervening_Seasons.svg

As the Earth orbits the sun, the days get longer and the nights become shorter for the hemisphere that is tilting towards the sun. At the halfway point neither hemisphere is tilted towards or away from the Sun. The days and nights are (almost) equal length. This date is called the **Equinox** from the Latin, *aequus* (equal) and *nox* (night).

For the northern hemisphere, the Spring Equinox is usually the 20th of March and the Autumn Equinox is usually the 22nd September.

Why do we get Moon Phases?

Over the course of a month, the moon looks a little different, changing from a crescent moon to a full moon and back to a crescent. The changing shapes that the Moon appears to take are called phases. A complete cycle of phases is known as a lunar month. The Moon takes around 29.5 days to make a complete orbit of the Earth.

https://commons.wikimedia.org/wiki/File:Moon_phases_en.jpg

A common misconception is that the phases of the moon are caused by the Earth's shadow (Osbourne et al, 1994). In fact, these phases are caused by the relative position of the Moon and the Earth and how we see the moon being lit from the Sun. Our view of the Moon changes as it orbits the Earth. This video explains more: https://youtu.be/wz01pTvuMa0

THE EARTH IN SPACE

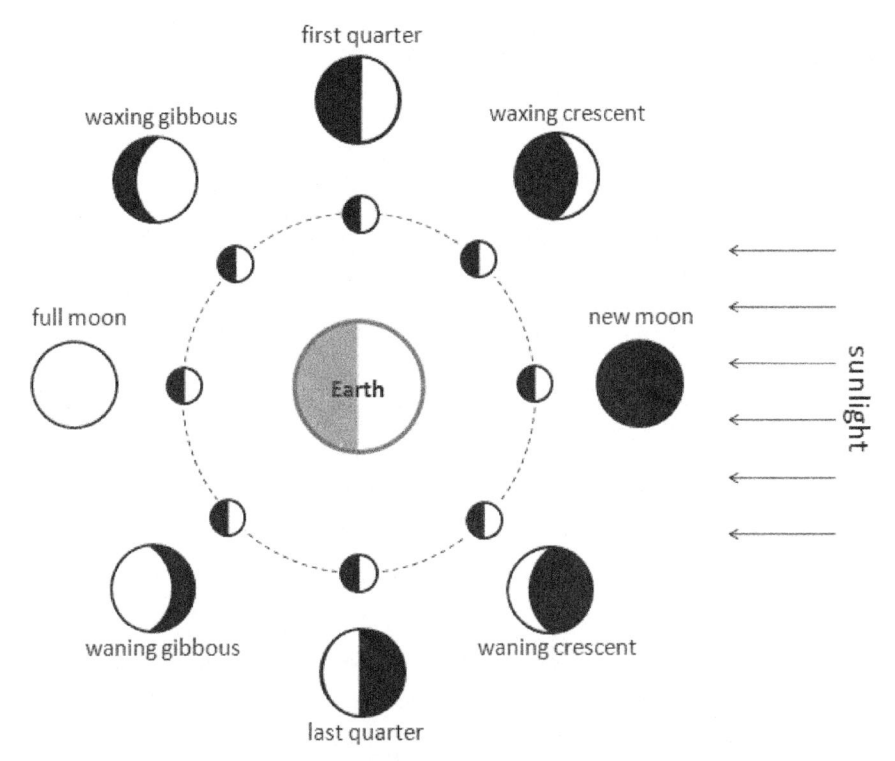

https://simple.wikipedia.org/wiki/Phases_of_the_Moon#/media/File:Moon_Phase_Diagram_for_Simple_English_Wikipedia.GIF

As the Moon orbits, light from the Sun is reflected by the Moon's surface. When the Earth is directly between the Sun and the Moon, we see a full moon. This is because the side of the Moon reflecting sunlight is facing us.

When the Moon is further on in its orbit, and less reflected light is visible, we see a last quarter moon. When the Moon moves between the Sun and the Earth, we see no Moon at all, as the side reflecting sunlight is facing away from the Earth. This is called a new moon.

So even though it looks like the Moon is changing shape over the course of a month, it is not. The changing phases are caused by the Moon's orbit around Earth, which changes the Moon's position relative to the Earth and Sun. (Read More Here: https://www.sciencefix.co.uk/2020/01/big-questions-why-do-we-get-moon-phases/)

You can model this in the classroom with a torch and a ball as outlined by NASA https://www.jpl.nasa.gov/edu/teach/activity/moon-phases/ , or you could use a ball with one half painted black.

You could also explore this using an online simulator like this https://ccnmtl.github.io/astro-simulations/lunar-phase-simulator/ Drag the moon around the Earth to see how the moon phase changes.

Eclipses

The Sun is about 400 times further away from us than the Moon, and it's also about 400 times bigger than the Moon. This strange cosmic coincidence means that both appear the same size in our sky and is also the reason we get lunar and solar eclipses.

When the Moon comes directly between the Earth and the Sun, we get a **solar eclipse**.

When the Earth comes directly between the moon and the Sun, we get a **lunar eclipse**. You could model this with a penny and a football. Place a football a short distance away. Hold the penny in front of your eye and try and move it until it exactly blocks the football. The ratio of the distance between the eye and the penny to the eye and the ball, should be the same ratio as the diameter of the penny to the football.

This video explains more: https://youtu.be/ljwZMYy930s

Stars, Planets, Galaxies

This topic area has a lot of important words and definitions to be introduced to the children. Here's an overview of some of the main ones.

Our sun is a **star**. It is exactly the same as all the stars they see in the night sky, but it is a lot closer. A star is a massive ball of extremely hot, luminous gas (plasma) that is held together by its own gravity.

Orbiting the sun are **planets**. These are large round balls of rock or gas. We live on one of these planets, called Earth. Some of these planets have **moons** that orbit them.

Also orbiting the sun are smaller balls of rock that are not quite planets, called **dwarf planets**. There are also smaller lumps of rock called **asteroids** and balls of ice known as **comets**. The sun, plus all of these things that orbit it are called a **Solar system.**

A group of stars is known as a **galaxy**. The galaxy that we are a part of is called the Milky Way. It contains around 300 billion stars. There are estimated to be over 100 billion galaxies in our universe. The universe contains everything that exists; the entire contents of space, including planets, moons, stars, comets, asteroids and space dust, all physical matter and energy.

The Solar System

A **solar system** is the name given to a star with planets orbiting around it. For us, it's the 8 planets that orbit our Sun, along with dwarf planets and asteroids.

The 8 planets are Mercury, Venus, Earth, Mars, Jupiter, Saturn, Uranus and Neptune

There are also 5 dwarf planets, these are called Ceres, Pluto, Haumea, Makemake and Eris. Dwarf planets have not cleared their orbits of other objects and so are not considered true planets. This is why Pluto was downgraded (See BBC 2015 for more https://www.bbc.co.uk/news/science-environment-33462184 and https://youtu.be/fIp4Ay1_-mI).

One of the best places to find out about all the planets and dwarf planets is the NASA Solar System website: https://solarsystem.nasa.gov/

https://commons.wikimedia.org/wiki/File:Planets2013.svg

Solar System Models

There are many different guides out there to help you model the solar system on a playground or school field. Some scale the size of the planets too, others keep them large to make them easier to see. Here are a few examples.

- Schoolyard Solar System: https://nssdc.gsfc.nasa.gov/planetary/education/schoolyard_ss/
- Solar System in my Pocket: https://www.ogdentrust.com/resources/phizzi-practical-solar-system-in-my-pocket
- Toilet roll solar system: https://www.iop.org/explore-physics/at-home/episode-11-toilet-roll-solar-system

A computer simulation such as Solar System Scope (https://www.solarsystemscope.com/) would also be a good tool to allow the pupils to explore how the planets move in relation to the sun and to each other. They could use it to work out the length of a year on different planets.

What is a Light Year?

In the light unit children will have learned that light travels very fast. The speed of light is 299, 792, 458 m/s. We're used to switching on a light and there being no delay for the light to reach us. The distances involved when talking about space are huge. So big in fact that it will take light time to cover those distances. For example, it will take light roughly 8 minutes to travel from the Sun to the Earth. It would take 18 years to fly that distance in an airplane.

When talking about distances in space, scientists use the term Light Year. This is the distance that light travels in a year. A light year is approximately 10 trillion kilometres, that's 10,000,000,000,000km!

The closest star to Earth (apart from our Sun) is called Proxima Centauri. It is a distance of 4. 2 light years away. That means the light takes just over 4 years to reach us. The Northern Star, Polaris is 434 light years away. So, when you are looking at it, you are seeing light that left the star 434 years ago.

Our nearest neighbouring galaxy, Andromeda is about 2.5 million light years away. If you were looking at Andromeda through a telescope, you would see it as it looked 2.5million years ago with light that began its journey when our ancient ancestors were just learning how to make stone tools!

Useful Links

BBC (2015) Why Is Pluto no longer a planet? https://www.bbc.co.uk/news/science-environment-33462184

IOP: Toilet Roll Solar System https://www.iop.org/explore-physics/at-home/episode-11-toilet-roll-solar-system#gref

Lunar Phase Simulator: https://ccnmtl.github.io/astro-simulations/lunar-phase-simulator/

NASA Solar System: https://solarsystem.nasa.gov/

Nasa. Moon Phases Classroom Activity: https://www.jpl.nasa.gov/edu/

teach/activity/moon-phases/

Ogden Trust. Research Cards. Earth and Space: https://www.ogdentrust.com/resources/research-cards-earth-and-space

Ogden Trust: Solar System in my Pocket: https://www.ogdentrust.com/resources/phizzi-practical-solar-system-in-my-pocket

Osbourne, J., Wadsworth, P., Black, P. and Meadows, J. (1994) SPACE Project Research Report: The Earth in Space https://www.stem.org.uk/elibrary/resource/29214

Scale of the Universe https://htwins.net/scale2/

Sherrington, T., (2021) My favourite CPD question for weaving teaching concepts and strategies together. https://teacherhead.com/2021/06/06/my-favourite-cpd-question-for-weaving-teaching-concepts-and-strategies-together/

Sun Earth and Moon Papercraft Model: https://www.sciencefix.co.uk/2019/07/quick-science-idea-sun-earth-and-moon-papercraft-model/

Schoolyard Solar System: https://nssdc.gsfc.nasa.gov/planetary/education/schoolyard_ss/

Solar System to Scale: https://youtu.be/zR3Igc3Rhfg

Solar System Scope: https://www.solarsystemscope.com/

The Kid Should See This: Why do leaves change colour? https://thekidshouldseethis.com/post/why-do-leaves-change-color

Why aren't there eclipses every month? https://youtu.be/ljwZMYy930s

Why do we always see the same face of the moon? https://www.sciencefix.co.uk/2020/06/why-do-we-always-see-the-same-face-of-the-moon/

Why do we get moon phases? https://www.sciencefix.co.uk/2020/01/big-questions-why-do-we-get-moon-phases/

9

Electricity

What is electricity?

Children will have regular experiences with electricity every day of their lives. They will know that televisions and games consoles will not work unless they are plugged in. Many toys need batteries to work, and children should be aware that batteries come in all different shapes and sizes. Batteries are a good introduction to voltage and the size of the "push" around a circuit.

Most children will know that phones and tablet computers in the home need charging from time to time. They might know that there are batteries inside and that they need to be plugged into the mains to recharge.

At a primary level, the explanation for electricity should be simplified a little from the one used in KS3 and above. Electricity is the flow of tiny, charged particles (called electrons). The size of the flow is called the **current**. The pupils can think of it like water flowing down a river, the faster the flow of water, the bigger the current.

Electricity can only flow when a power supply is able to "push" the electrons around a complete circuit. This means a path is needed from the power supply, through the components in the circuit, and back to the power supply. The size of the push is called the **voltage**. The higher the voltage, the bigger the push moving the electrons around the circuit.

Electrons are not introduced to pupils until year 10. So, for primary it might be wise to talk about small particles that carry something called "charge" (Chapman, 2014). These charged particles moving around the wires produces electricity.

Electricity is a form of energy. It can be converted by circuit components, such as light bulbs, motors and buzzers, into other useful forms of energy.

Conductors and Insulators

A conductor is a material that allows energy (heat or electricity) to pass through it easily. Metals are good conductors because their electrons are free to move from one atom to the next and take the energy with them. Wires are often made of copper because it is a good conductor of electricity.

One common non-metal that is a conductor is graphite. The "lead" from a pencil (which is actually graphite) will conduct electricity. Sharpen both ends of a pencil to make it easier to attach the clips. If the pencil has been dropped, and there's a crack in the lead then it may not work. They could also try a piece of graphite from a propelling (mechanical) pencil instead.

An insulator is a material that does not allow electricity, heat or sound to pass through it easily. The electrons in insulators are not free to move or to carry energy from one atom to the next. Rubber, plastic and wood are all insulators.

Circuits

For electricity to flow, a complete circuit is needed. If there is a gap in the circuit, electricity won't flow.

For a simple demonstration with a class, an Energy Stick is a great gadget to have handy. (See https://www.sciencefix.co.uk/2019/05/teaching-circuits-with-an-energy-stick/). Stand the whole class in a circle, holding hands. Put the energy stick between two of the pupils, one holding each end. The stick should flash and buzz showing there's a circuit being made.

Ask different pairs of pupils to let go of their hands. They'll break the circuit, and the stick will go quiet.

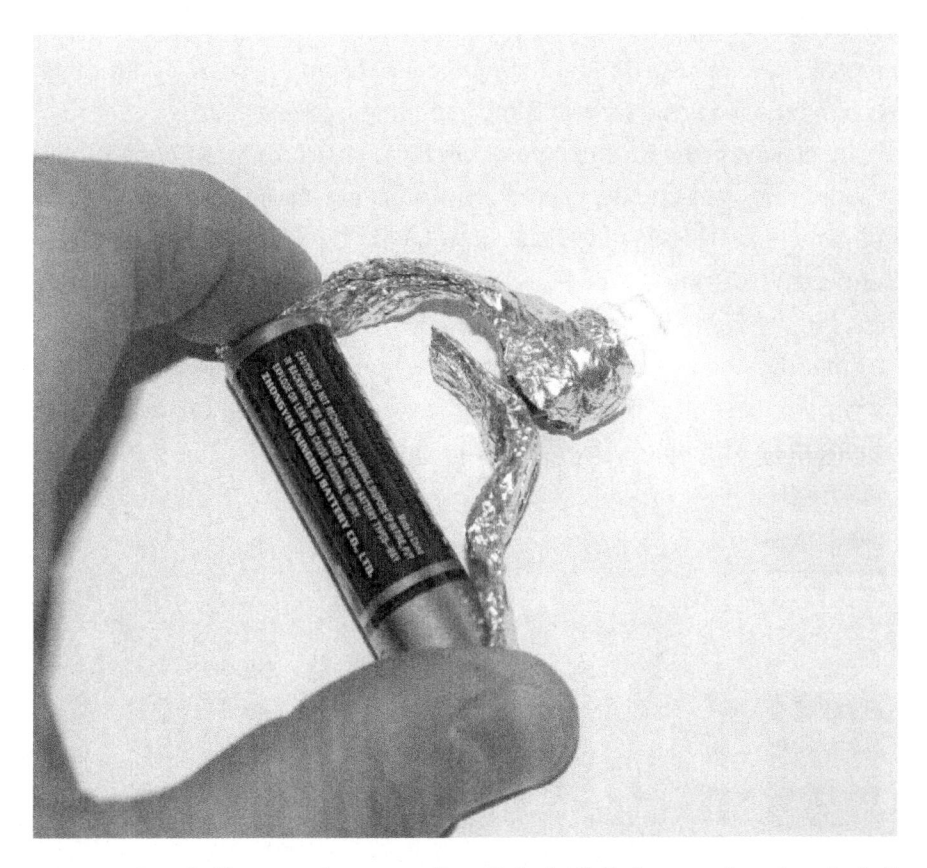

You can also challenge a class to make a light bulb light up only using tin foil and a battery. It's not as easy as it looks.

For this to work they will need to tear the foil into two strips. Have one strip coming from one end of the battery to the side of the metal at the base of the bulb. The other piece of tin foil should run from the other end of the batter to the very bottom of the bulb. This should create a circuit through the bulb.

Take care not to let them just connect the two ends of the battery with foil as it can get hot!

Series Circuits

The simplest circuit is known as a series circuit. In this type of circuit each component is connected one after the other, so the current has to pass through each in turn and is the same at every point in the circuit.

One disadvantage of this type of circuit is that if one component fails, creating an open circuit, current will not flow through the rest of the components. This would create a problem if, for example, bulbs were connected in series. If one bulb were to fail the others would also switch off.

Similarly, each of the bulbs could not be controlled individually as a switch would stop current flowing in the entire circuit. For this reason, the applications of simple series circuits are limited

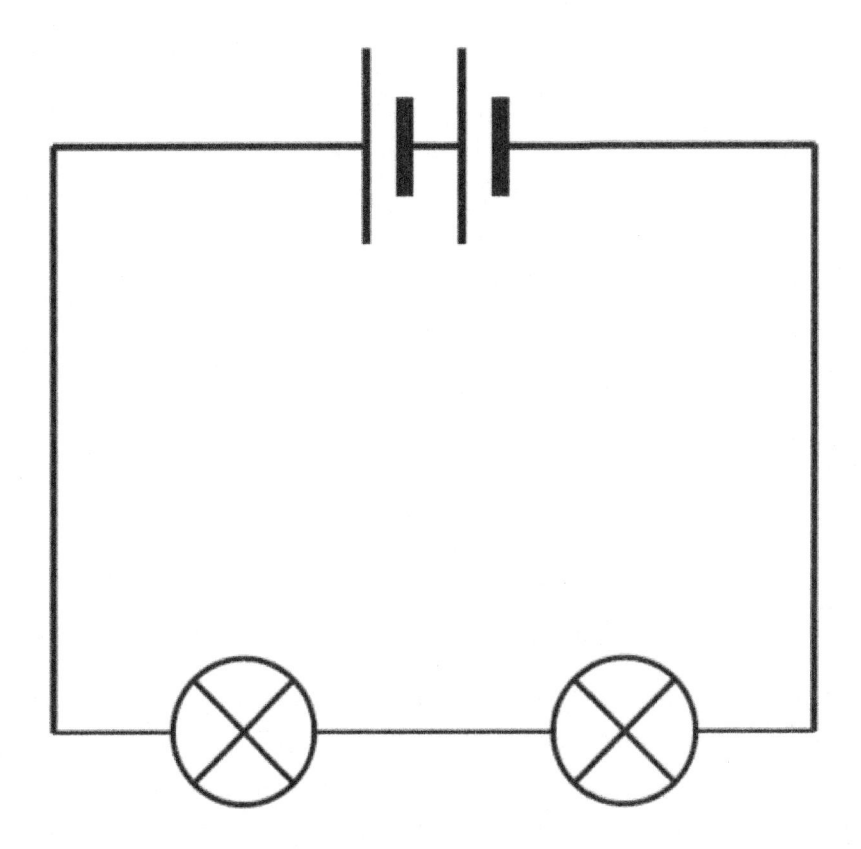

A **Short circuit** is a path in a circuit that contains no components. In a short circuit, there is very little resistance to the flow of electricity therefore the current will take this path around the circuit

Bulbs and Batteries

When you add more light bulbs to a series circuit, the brightness of the bulbs should decrease. This is because the battery provides a specific amount of energy to the electrons linked to the voltage of the battery. As the electrons flow around a circuit, they provide the components with electrical energy and the bulbs convert this electrical energy into light (and heat) energy.

The available energy is shared between all the components. The more bulbs there are in the circuit, the less energy is available for each one, and the dimmer the bulbs become.

Changing the voltage of the battery also affects the brightness of the bulbs. As the voltage increases, the energy provided to the electrons also increases. The larger the amount of electrical energy supplied, the brighter the bulbs will be.

To Do: If you have the equipment, make a simple circuit with a battery and a bulb and put different materials into the circuit to see if the bulb lights up. Sort materials into conductors and insulators in this way. If you don't have access to the right equipment, try the Phet simulator at https://phet.colorado.edu/sims/html/circuit-construction-kit-dc/latest/circuit-construction-kit-dc_en.html

Drawing Circuits

In Year 4, the pupils are just expected to draw circuits how they look – with wiggly wires and batteries and bulbs drawn how they are. In Year 6 the pupils are expected to draw circuits using the more scientific symbols and straight lines. For a guide to this, visit: https://www.bbc.co.uk/bitesize/topics/zq99q6f/articles/zs7g4j6

The basic symbols they are expected to draw are as follows:

Battery · Wire · Bulb · Buzzer

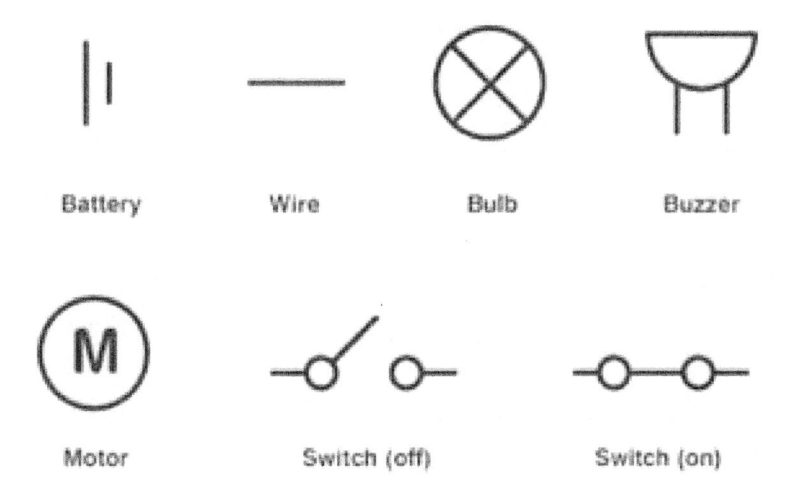

Motor · Switch (off) · Switch (on)

Chapman (2014) suggests building the real circuit on a large sheet of sugar paper alongside the circuit diagram, so pupils can see how the real circuit relates to the diagram.

Models and analogies in electricity

What is actually going on inside a circuit? It's impossible to see, and to explain it properly uses concepts way above primary school level. So how can we explain it? Time for a model!

Electricity is an abstract idea. We can see its effect on something like a light bulb, but it is very hard to understand what is happening inside a circuit.

To help understand what is going on, we need to use models or analogies. To use another frame of reference to help describe something. For example, many people think about electricity in terms of something else - water flowing through pipes or traffic moving along roads. See Asoko (1995)

Analogies as pedagogical tools each have their own strengths and limitations (Ramos 2011). But they have potential if they are properly used. Often one analogy won't be enough. Chiu et al (2005) used two electrical analogies with one group of children and a single analogy to another group. Although each model had weaknesses, found that presenting children with several analogies aided their learning and understanding of how a circuit works.

Here are a few suggestions for models that could be used to help pupils begin to understand electricity:

Water Pump

Imagine that the wires are pipes and filled with water. The pump is the battery. The pump switches on and pushes the water around the pipes. This is the flow of electricity, which we call current. The strength of the pump is the voltage – the bigger the push, the faster the water flows around the pipes and the bigger the current.

A water wheel represents a component such as a bulb. The faster the current, the faster the water wheel moves (the brighter the bulb)

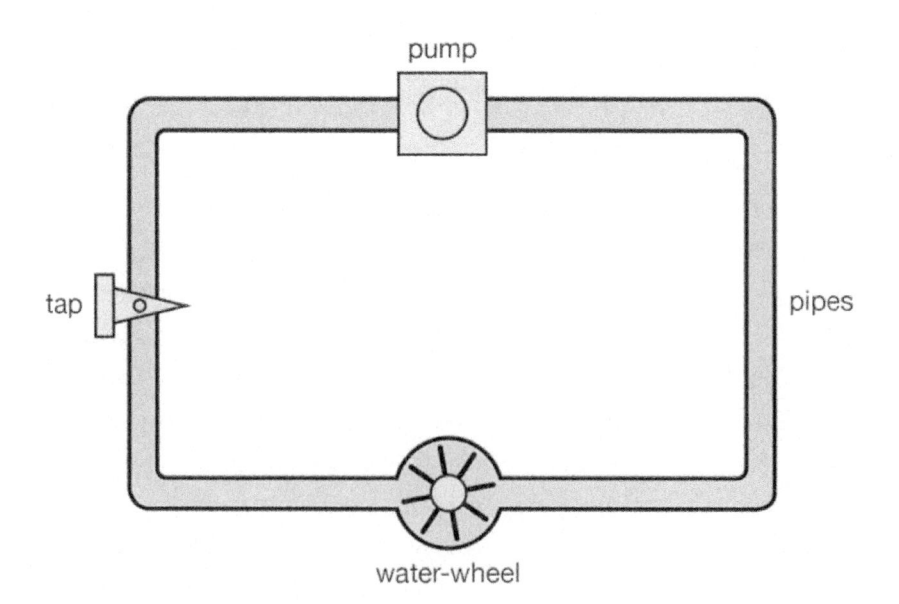

See: https://www.iop.org/sites/default/files/2019-11/Electric-circuits.ppt

String Loop Model

Use a small group of pupils and ask them to sit in a circle on the floor. Use a loop of string (or a hoop). Have them hold their hands out so that the string can pass between their thumb and forefinger. One child can then act as the battery, they start moving the string around in a circle. The string is the current, flowing around in a circuit. See this guide from the IOP for more detail (https://spark.iop.org/rope-loop-electric-circuit-model)

Sweetie Circle

The pupils stand in a circle with a plate of sweets at one end and a hoop at the other. The pupils walk around in a circle and as they pass the bowl, they should take a sweet. When they reach the hoop, they should eat the sweet and climb through the hoop (or do a star jump). They then return around the other side of the circle and back to the bowl.

In this model the pupils are the current and the plate of sweets is the battery. The sweets are the energy, which they use up in climbing through the hoop (the bulb) or doing the star jump.

Model railway

Ask the pupils to think about a model railway track set up as a simple loop. The train loads its goods at the station (the battery), delivers them to the factory (the bulb) and then returns to the station. In this model the tracks are the wires, and the train is the current.

No model is perfect, they will usually fall down on some aspect of what actually happens inside a circuit. But the shortfalls could be discussed with the pupils. Pupils will need support in using any analogy to aid their understanding. The relationship between the parts of the model and what is being explained needs to be made explicit for them to make sense of the science behind the model (Ramos 2011).

For more analogies, see Asoko (1995) https://www.tes.com/news/faulty-connections

Electrical Safety

It is important to take precautions when using electricity and teach children about the dangers. Children should be taught to never touch exposed wires. They should never leave liquids next to electrical appliances or operate with wet hands. Always switch lights off at the mains before changing light bulbs. Switch off all electrical appliances before you leave the house or go to bed.

Explain the dangers of overhead power lines – be careful when flying kites or climbing trees near power lines, when carrying long fishing lines. They should be warned about going near transformers in electrical substations or electrified railway lines.

Where does electricity come from?

Most of the electricity we use is created in power stations. The current leaves the power station through power lines and cables, to reach our homes, our schools and our workplaces. This type of electricity is called mains electricity.

At the heart of all power stations are turbines and generators. A turbine is a machine that rotates as a fluid passes over or through it. Turbines are often connected to a generator in order to convert this energy of movement into electricity.

A generator is a machine that turns kinetic energy into electricity by using a spinning magnet. A dynamo light on a bike is a good example of a simple generator. As the pedals and wheels turn, they spin a magnet that produces enough electricity to power the light on the bike. The generator in a power station or a wind turbine are just giant versions of a dynamo.

Typically, the energy from fossil fuels or nuclear energy is used to boil water and the steam makes the turbines move. Some forms of energy use wind or moving water to make the turbines move.

Renewable Energy

Solar cells are devices that convert light energy directly into electrical energy. Solar cells are also known as photovoltaic cells. Small electrical devices, such as calculators, often use solar cells. Larger devices can also be powered by solar cells; this technology has become cheaper and more efficient.

Some **solar panels** contain water that is heated directly by sunlight. Large panels are able to generate steam that can be used to turn turbines and generate electricity. On a smaller scale, panels are used directly as a source of hot water.

Wind power uses turbines with large blades like a windmill. These are moved by the wind to generate electricity.

Geothermal Power uses the heat energy from deep beneath the Earth's surface. The steam produced from hot springs and geysers can be used to turn turbines that drive generators to produce electricity.

Hydroelectric power creates electricity from moving water. Falling water from dams and waterfalls, other fast flowing water and tidal movement can be used to drive a turbine to turn a generator and produce electricity.

Application of Electricity – things to make and do

As stated in the National Curriculum, year 6 builds on the work in year 4. "Pupils should construct simple series circuits, to help them to answer questions about what happens when they try different components, for example, switches, bulbs, buzzers and motors."

Pupils should also be able to use their knowledge to design and make useful circuits – such as burglar alarms or traffic lights. Obviously, there are some good links to make to Design and Technology here.

These useful circuits all allow the pupils to apply their knowledge of circuits to design different things. Here are some links to a few resources to give you some ideas of what can be made:

- Traffic Lights: https://www.sfi.ie/site-files/primary-science/media/pdfs/col/dpsm_traffic_lights_activity.pdf
- Operation Game: https://www.instructables.com/id/Giant-Game-of-Operation/
- Buzz Wire Game: https://www.instructables.com/id/Buzz-Wire-Kit/
- Burglar Alarm: https://www.electronics-notes.com/articles/basic_concepts/stem-projects-activities/how-to-build-burglar-alarm.php
- Paper Circuits: https://www.exploratorium.edu/tinkering/projects/paper-circuits

Telegraphs and Morse Code

Imagine a circuit with a simple switch and a buzzer. When the switch is closed, the buzzer sounds. Now imagine that this circuit is really long, the switch is in one town, and the buzzer is in another town. That's basically how the telegraph system worked back in the 1840s. Using morse code, messages could be sent, letter by letter, much faster than via the postal service. There was even a wire laid under the Atlantic to allow messages to be sent from Europe to America.

Pupils could explore morse code and send simple messages to each other. This would link nicely to a topic on The Victorians or Codebreaking.

What is Lightning?

Have ever heard a crackle or noticed little sparks of light when removing a jumper? Perhaps you have received a "shock" after touching a metal surface or another person. These shocks are the result of static electricity.

Lightning is also a type of static electricity. But the force of lightning is much more powerful.

Lightning is created in a thundercloud when small bits of ice bump into each other as they move. All of those collisions make static electrical charges in the clouds.

When you rub some materials, it can cause electrons to move from one material to the other. This means that the material that loses electrons becomes positively charged and the material that gains electrons becomes negatively charged

Just like a battery, these clouds have a positive and a negative end. The positive charges are at the top of the cloud and negative charges are at the bottom. When the negative charge at the bottom gets strong enough, the cloud releases energy, and lightning strikes!

The lightning travels through the air and because opposites attract, it is attracted to a place that has the opposite charge. This could be another cloud or the ground.

Although exciting to watch, lightning can be very dangerous. One bolt of lightning contains enough energy to toast 100,000 pieces of bread.

Try this static electricity simulator from Phet https://phet.colorado.edu/en/simulations/balloons-and-static-electricity

Useful Links

Asoko, H., (2005) Faulty Connections: https://www.tes.com/news/faulty-connections

Azaiza, Ibtesam & Bar, Varda & Awad, Yaser. (2012). Pupils' Explanations of Natural Phenomena and Their Relationship to Electricity. Creative Education. 03. 1354-1365. https://www.researchgate.net/publication/271293337_Pupils%27_Explanations_of_Natural_Phenomena_and_Their_Relationship_to_Electricity

BBC Bitesize. How do you draw electrical symbols and diagrams https://www.bbc.co.uk/bitesize/topics/zq99q6f/articles/zs7g4j6

Burglar Alarm: https://www.electronics-notes.com/articles/basic_concepts/stem-projects-activities/how-to-build-burglar-alarm.php

Buzz Wire Game: https://www.instructables.com/id/Buzz-Wire-Kit/

Chapman, S. (2013) Teaching the Big Ideas of Electricity at Primary Level. Primary Science. 135 https://www.ase.org.uk/resources/primary-science/issue-135/teaching-thebig-ideas-electricity-primary-level

Chiu, Mei-Hung & Lin, Jing-Wen. (2005). Promoting fourth graders' conceptual change of their understanding of electric current via multiple analogies. Journal of Research in Science Teaching. 42. 429 - 464. https://www.researchgate.net/publication/227658723_Promoting_fourth_graders%27_conceptual_change_of_their_understanding_of_electric_current_via_multiple_analogies

Glauert, E. (2009). How Young Pupils Understand Electric Circuits: Prediction, explanation and exploration. International Journal of Science Education. 31. https://discovery.ucl.ac.uk/id/eprint/10002194/

History.com: Morse Code and the Telegram https://www.history.com/topics/inventions/telegraph

Nicholson, D. (2019) Teaching Electricity with an Energy Stick see https://www.sciencefix.co.uk/2019/05/teaching-circuits-with-an-energy-stick/

Operation Game: https://www.instructables.com/id/Giant-Game-of-Operation/

Paper Circuits: https://www.exploratorium.edu/tinkering/projects/paper-circuits

Ramos, M., (2011). Analogies as tools for making meaning in elementary science education. How do they work in classroom settings? Eurasia Journal of Mathematics, Science and Technology. 7 pp29-29. https://www.ejmste.com/download/analogies-as-tools-for-meaningmaking-in-elementary-scienceeducation-how-do-they-work-inclassroom-4201.pdf

Science Museum: Titanic, Marconi and the Wireless Telegraph https://www.sciencemuseum.org.uk/objects-and-stories/titanic-marconi-and-wireless-telegraph

Space Project Research Report: Electricity https://www.stem.org.uk/resources/elibrary/resource/29215/space-project-research-report-electricity

Squishy Circuits: https://squishycircuits.com/

Scrappy Circuits: https://makezine.com/projects/scrappy-circuits/

Static Electricity: https://phet.colorado.edu/en/simulations/balloons-and-static-electricity

Traffic Lights: https://www.sfi.ie/site-files/primary-science/media/pdfs/col/dpsm_traffic_lights_activity.pdf

10

Light and Sound

What is Light?

Some important facts about light that you should know:

- Light is a form of energy that our eyes can see.
- Light travels in straight lines
- Light is very fast. The speed of light is roughly 300,000 kilometres per second. It takes light 8 minutes to get from the Sun to the earth.
- Light is able to travel through a vacuum
- We are able to see things because light rays bounce off objects and into our eyes.
- When light is blocked, it can cause a shadow
- Light from the sun can be dangerous. We should never look directly at the sun. Sunlight also includes ultraviolet light which can give us sunburn and damage our skin.

Exploring Light in EYFS

Young pupils can explore light as part of using their senses. Investigating light (and sound) can provide engaging and stimulating sensory experiences. Pupils could use a light table or an overhead projector to explore making patterns from different translucent objects such as plastic tiles, glass pebbles and acrylic shapes. A cheap light table can be made from a plastic storage box with white Christmas tree lights inside.

The teaching of light can also provide great cross curricular links with art and allow the pupils to express themselves creatively in different ways.

See Brunton and Thornton (2006) for more ideas https://www.nurseryworld.co.uk/features/article/early-years-science-light

Exploring Light in KS1

Although there is no longer a separate Light unit in KS1, there is plenty of scope to explore light within the Materials units. The pupils can explore transparent, opaque and translucent materials as a property of different materials. This means they can explore shadows and make shadow puppets for example. What would be the best material to make the shadow puppets from?

Light in KS2

Light is covered in Year 3 and again in Year 6. In year 3, the focus is on how we see things, how light is reflected and how shadows are formed. They should be taught about how sunlight can be dangerous and not to look directly at the sun. The emphasis here is on exploring and recognising the different phenomena.

In year 6 the focus in on light travelling in straight lines and how that can be used to explain how we see things and how shadows are made. They will have explored this in year 3, but now the emphasis is on explaining these phenomena.

LIGHT AND SOUND

When asked to explain how we see things, pupils may draw arrows coming out of a person's eyes and hitting objects (Space Project, 1994). Vision is seen as an active process where we are scanning for objects. Explain that we see because light from a light source bounces off objects and enters our eyes.

A good way to show that light travels in straight lines is to use three pieces of card with holes punched in the centres. Line them up so that when you shine a torch through the holes, you can see the spot of light on a screen or sheet of paper. If you move the middle card left or right a few centimetres, then the spot vanishes. The light can't bend around to move through all the holes, it can only travel through when they're all lined up. Watch this demonstration for more: https://www.bbc.co.uk/bitesize/clips/zyntsbk

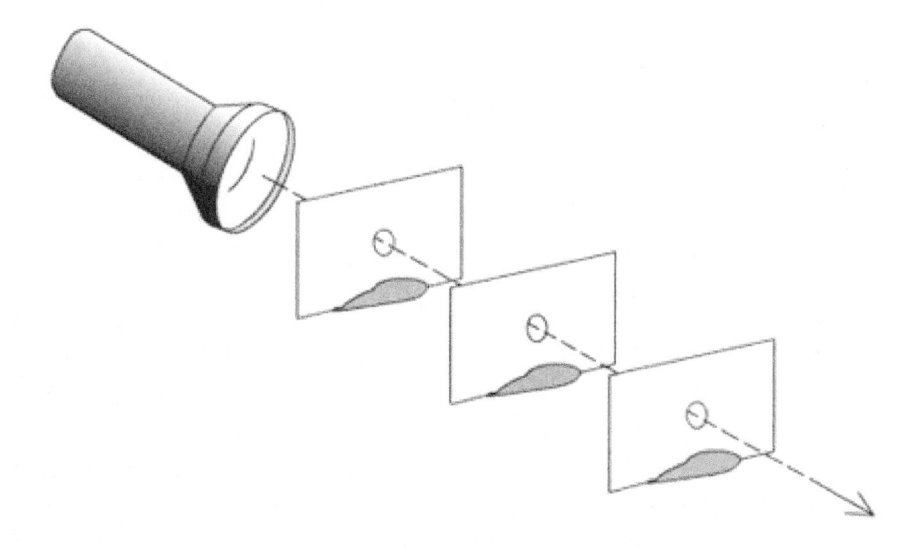

Mirrors

Reflection occurs when light bounces off a surface. All objects reflect at least some light. Shiny, smooth surfaces reflect lots of light in one direction, and are known as reflectors. Other objects with uneven surfaces scatter light in lots of different directions.

When a ray of light is reflected by a surface, the angle between the reflected ray and a line perpendicular to the surface at the point of reflection is known as the angle of reflection. The angle at which light strikes the surface is called the angle of incidence. These two angles should be exactly the same when light strikes a smooth surface like a mirror

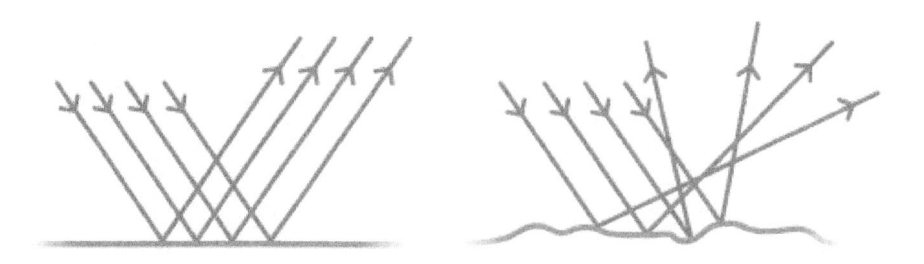

We can explore this to build things like periscopes using small mirrors and a cardboard tube. This allows us to look over objects or look around corners. To make your own, follow this guide to making a periscope: https://www.wikihow.com/Make-a-Periscope

Pupils could make their own kaleidoscopes by covering card with tin foil and then folding the card into a triangular prism. The pupils can then draw patterns on paper and see how they look through the kaleidoscope when it is pointed towards the light. Like this: https://www.tate.org.uk/kids/make/cut-paste/make-kaleidoscope

Pupils can also look at how things look in curved mirrors – a shiny metal spoon makes a good cheap curved mirror. The side of the spoon that curves outwards is a **convex** mirror and the side of the spoon that curves inwards is a **concave** mirror.

How do we get shadows and how do they change?

You'll have seen shadows all over the place. Long shadows on a summer evening, or the shadows of clouds as they pass by overhead. But how are they formed, and how can you explore them in a classroom?

When an object blocks the path of a beam of light a shadow is formed. Light travels in straight lines and cannot bend around an object in its path, so a dark area is produced which has the same shape as the object.

The size of a shadow depends on the distance between the light source and the object that is creating the shadow. When the light source is close to the object, a lot of light is blocked, and a large shadow is formed. When the object is far away, a smaller amount of light is blocked and so a smaller shadow is formed.

Opaque objects create dark shadows because they block all the light. Translucent objects, such as leaves, let a little light through so their shadows are not as dark as those created by opaque objects. Transparent objects, like water, let all light through and don't make any shadows at all.

This video explains more: https://www.bbc.co.uk/bitesize/clips/z8vfb9q

Investigating Shadows

To investigate shadows, you will need a torch, a ruler, a screen and an object to make the shadow. Small toys and dolls are good, or you could just use shapes cut out of card. A mini whiteboard makes a good screen as the pupils can mark lines straight onto it with whiteboard pens.

Ask the pupils to look at the relationship between the torch, the object and the screen. Keep the torch fixed and move the object, what is the relationship between the distance from the torch (or the screen) and the size of the shadow. Keep the object fixed and move the torch, what happens now?

You could make links to stories which mention shadows such as Peter Pan or The Gruffalo's Child. You could cut a mouse shape out of card to make the big bad mouse shadow, as explained here: https://www.sciencefix.co.uk/2020/03/gruffalos-child-shadow-puppets-investigation/

When covering this in year 6, you can link back to the Earth in Space unit from year 5. Pupils can explain why shadows are longer in the morning or evening, or why shadows are longer in the winter. Model this by moving the torch higher and lower in relation to the object.

To Do: Watch this video of Attraction performing a shadow show. https://youtu.be/a4Fv98jttYA?t=184 Pause it at the 3.14 mark. The shadow of the mum is twice the size of the daughter she's holding hands with. Can you explain how they did this when all the performers are of similar heights? Could you mock it up with two toys and a torch? How could you use this as an investigation stimulus?

What is Sound?

Sound is produced when something vibrates, like a guitar string or a loudspeaker. This makes the particles in the air vibrate, which makes the particles next to them vibrate, and so on. The sound wave spreads out like a ripple of vibrations, in the same way as ripples in a pond spread out when a stone is dropped into it.

Sound waves need a medium such as air, wood or water through which to travel. They cannot travel through a vacuum because there are no particles to pass on the energy. As the poster for Alien said, "In Space, No-one Can Hear You Scream." In reality, every space battle you see in the movies should be totally silent, as there is no air to carry the sound of the lasers and explosions.

String telephones work because the sound waves travel along the string. This works as long as the string is kept taut. If the string goes slack, it stops working. If you've never made a string telephone, follow this quick guide: https://youtu.be/4S7nG6S1isM

Travelling Sounds

Sound waves carry energy from one place to another by moving the medium they travel through. The waves move the medium as a series of **compressions** where the molecules move together and **rarefactions** where they are spread further apart. The energy travels in the same direction as the movement of the wave. This is called a longitudinal wave.

Sound Waves are hard to visualise and are hard to explain clearly in a diagram. You can model the movement of a sound wave using a slinky spring. This provides a good visual demonstration of how the particles transmit the vibrations to each other along the slinky.

Watch this video for more: **https://youtu.be/xOAsekn-NTQ**

Use a hard, smooth surface such as a desk or the floor. Have a child hold the other end of the slinky. Quickly move one end forwards and backwards so the compressions move along the length of the slinky. Point out that the coils don't move along the spring – they just move forwards then backwards, but they make the next coil move, and the next. So, the wave passes along the spring.

What do Pupils Think?

When asked to show how sound travels from an object such as a bell to our ears the pupils might draw sounds travelling as musical notes, probably having seen similar in comics or cartoons (Space Report, 1990). Pupils might think that sounds travel in straight lines, from the sound source to their ears. This is probably a result of being taught that this is how light travels.

To demonstrate that sounds travel in all directions, ask the children to sit in a circle and put an alarm clock or a ringing phone in the middle of the circle. Can they all hear it? Explain to them that the sound must be travelling from the sound source in all directions. You could also use a flat tray of water and drop a small pebble into it. They can see the waves moving out in a circle.

Marvin and Milo: Sound Experiments

The Institute of Physics has a series of cartoons featuring Marvin and Milo with ideas for simple experiments you can carry out in class, or at home. Here are some good ones related to sound to try out for yourself:

Musical Coat Hanger: https://spark.iop.org/collections/marvin-and-milo#musical-coat-hanger

Bottle Blowing: https://spark.iop.org/collections/marvin-and-milo#bottle-blowing

Screech: https://spark.iop.org/collections/marvin-and-milo#screech

Loud Lollies: https://spark.iop.org/collections/marvin-and-milo#loud-lollies

Sound in EYFS and KS1

There are lots of opportunities for exploring sound in EYFS. Like light, there are lots of opportunities to explore it in the context of our senses. It also links nicely to music. Pupils can use musical instruments and explore how different sounds are made. They could make their own shakers out of plastic pots and rice. They can listen carefully to sounds such as https://www.bbc.co.uk/teach/school-radio/eyfs-listening-skills/zbc4y9q. See Brunton & Thornton (2006) for more ideas.

Like Light, Sound does not have a specific unit in KS1, but pupils could investigate soundproofing as a property of a material. For example, they could make links to books such as Peace at Last by Jill Murphy. Could the pupils choose the best material to make some earmuffs for Mr Bear?

Investigating Sound – changing pitch and volume

To make sound waves easier for us to visualise, they are often drawn as a sine wave, like a light wave or ocean wave. The forward/back movement of the wave is converted into an up/down curve instead.

The distance from peak to peak is called the wavelength. The height is called the amplitude.

Whilst it is easier to draw them like this, it is important not to mix this up with the way that the sound waves move.

The **pitch** of a sound refers to whether it is perceived as high or low in tone. Pitch depends on how frequently the vibrations are made by the source.

Imagine you were standing in one spot and could see the waves passing by. The frequency of a sound is the number of waves that passes by in one second. So, if 10 waves pass by the frequency is 10Hz. If 100 waves pass by the frequency is 100Hz

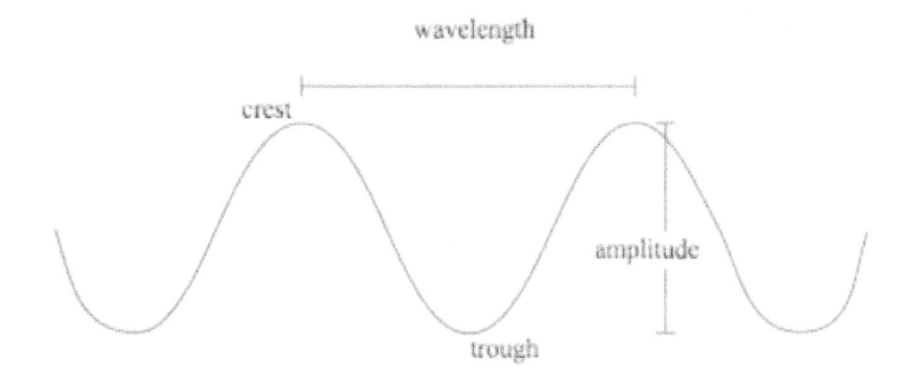

Exploring Pitch

Musicians change the pitch of their instruments in different ways. The strings of an instrument can be tuned by tightening them. Tightening makes them vibrate at a higher frequency creating a higher-pitched note, while loosening the strings creates a lower-pitched note. By moving their finger along a guitar string a guitarist can effectively make the vibrating section of the string longer or shorter. Shorter strings vibrate faster than longer strings, so the pitch of the note changes. In wind instruments, the length and volume of the air column affect pitch. These videos from the BBC explain more: https://www.bbc.co.uk/teach/class-clips-video/music—science-ks2-house-of-sound/zncr7nb

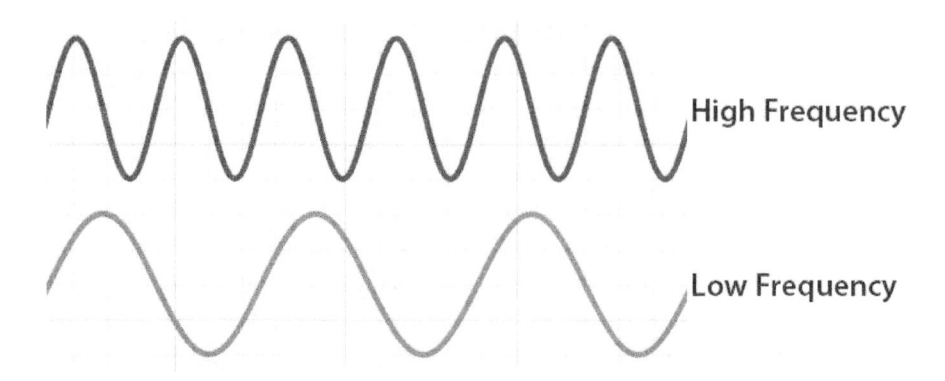

Hang a ruler over the edge of a desk. Change how much of the ruler is hanging over the edge. Experiment and see what happens. The longer the length of ruler hanging over the edge, the slower it will vibrate and the lower the note. See here for a demo: https://youtu.be/4SpSwTvbZI4

You could also make a straw flute – cut a drinking straw to a point at one end, flatten it, then blow. Change the length of the straw by cutting a cm or so from the end each time and see what happens to the pitch. See here for more; https://www.fizzicseducation.com.au/150-science-experiments/light-sound-experiments/make-a-straw-flute/

Amplitude and Volume

The amplitude of the wave is how far it vibrates forwards and backwards. On a graph it can be shown as the distance from the midpoint to the top of the wave.

In a quiet sound, the amplitude is small. The wave doesn't move much and has a small amount of energy. In a loud sound, the amplitude is high. The wave moves a lot and has a lot of energy.

A bigger vibration, caused by plucking a string, blowing harder or hitting an object with greater intensity, increases volume. The larger the vibration, the more energy it has and the louder the sound.

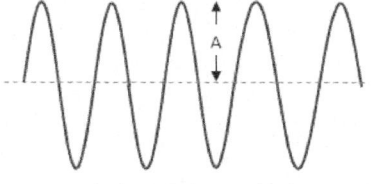

A loud sound – large amplitude

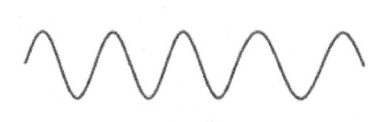

A soft (quiet) sound – small amplitude

How do we hear?

We hear sounds because our ear acts as a receiver. The vibrations in the air reach us and are gathered by the outer ear. The sound is funnelled down the ear canal and makes the eardrum vibrate.

The vibrations are then transfer via three small bones called the ossicles to the cochlea. The cochlea is filled with liquid and nerve cells. The vibrations in the liquid are picked up by these hair cells and sent as impulses along the auditory nerve to the brain which translates the messages into a sensation of sound.

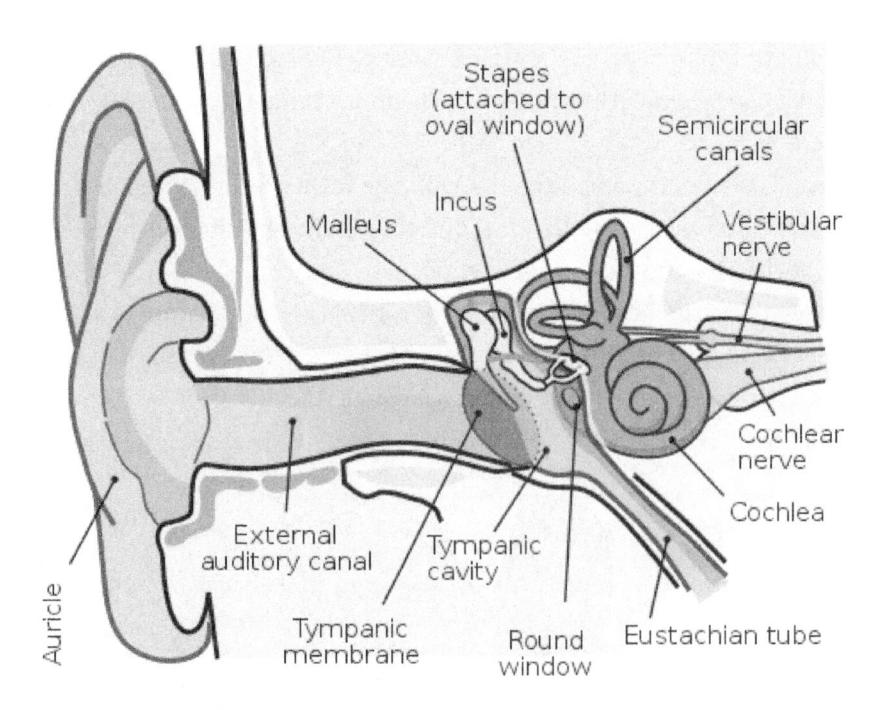

https://commons.wikimedia.org/wiki/File:Anatomy_of_the_Human_Ear.svg

How High Can You Hear?

You can use a tone generator (such as https://www.szynalski.com/tone-generator/) to generate sounds of different frequencies. Start with a low frequency and gradually make it higher, increasing the pitch of the sound.

Ask pupils to put their hands up when they can no longer hear the sound. At frequencies of around 18-20KHz they should begin to stop hearing the sound. They should be able to hear higher sounds than any adults in the classroom!

Useful Links

BBC Bitesize: Where does light and shade come from? https://www.bbc.co.uk/bitesize/clips/z8vfb9q

BBC House of Sound: https://www.bbc.co.uk/teach/class-clips-video/music—science-ks2-house-of-sound/zncr7nb

Brunton, P., & Thornton, L., (2006) Early Years Science: Light. Nursery World https://www.nurseryworld.co.uk/features/article/early-years-science-light

Brunton, P., & Thornton, L., (2006) Early Years Science: Sound. Nursery World https://www.nurseryworld.co.uk/features/article/early-years-science-sound

Gruffalo's Child Shadow Puppets Investigation https://www.sciencefix.co.uk/2020/03/gruffalos-child-shadow-puppets-investigation/

How does the ear work? https://rnid.org.uk/information-and-support/ear-health/how-the-ear-works/

Make a straw flute: https://www.fizzicseducation.com.au/150-science-experiments/light-sound-experiments/make-a-straw-flute/

Make a string telephone: https://youtu.be/4S7nG6S1isM

Marvin and Milo: https://spark.iop.org/collections/marvin-and-milo

Science of Sound: https://www.scholastic.com/teachers/articles/teaching-content/science-sound/

Space Project Research Project Light https://www.stem.org.uk/resources/elibrary/resource/29216/space-project-research-report-light

Space Research Report (1990): Sound https://www.stem.org.uk/resources/elibrary/resource/29213/space-project-research-report-sound

Tate Kids: Make a Kaleidoscope https://www.tate.org.uk/kids/make/cut-paste/make-kaleidoscope

Wikihow: Make a Periscope https://www.wikihow.com/Make-a-Periscope

11

What is Science and Working Scientifically?

Science and the Scientific Method

Pupils should be inspired by their first formal educational encounters with science at primary school (Wellcome, 2014). Primary science should develop pupils' understanding of the world, nurture their curiosity and teach essential skills, including enquiry, observation, prediction, analysis, reasoning and explanation.

Scientific Enquiry describes the processes and skills pupils should be taught and use, to find out more about the world and how it works (ASE 2018).

What is the scientific method?

At a very basic level, science is about being inquisitive and asking "why?". The role of science is to explain the world around us the best that we can, using all the available evidence.

The scientific method is an important way of thinking. It starts with a question, for example "Why does something happen the way it does?". This might lead to a prediction of what they think might happen. An experiment could then be carried out, in which this prediction is tested, and evidence is collected. A judgement is then made as to whether the evidence is strong enough to support or reject the prediction. This in turn might generate new questions, that can also be tested. There are many ways to carry out a practical enquiry, and we'll look at those a little later.

In the primary classroom, the process could look like this:

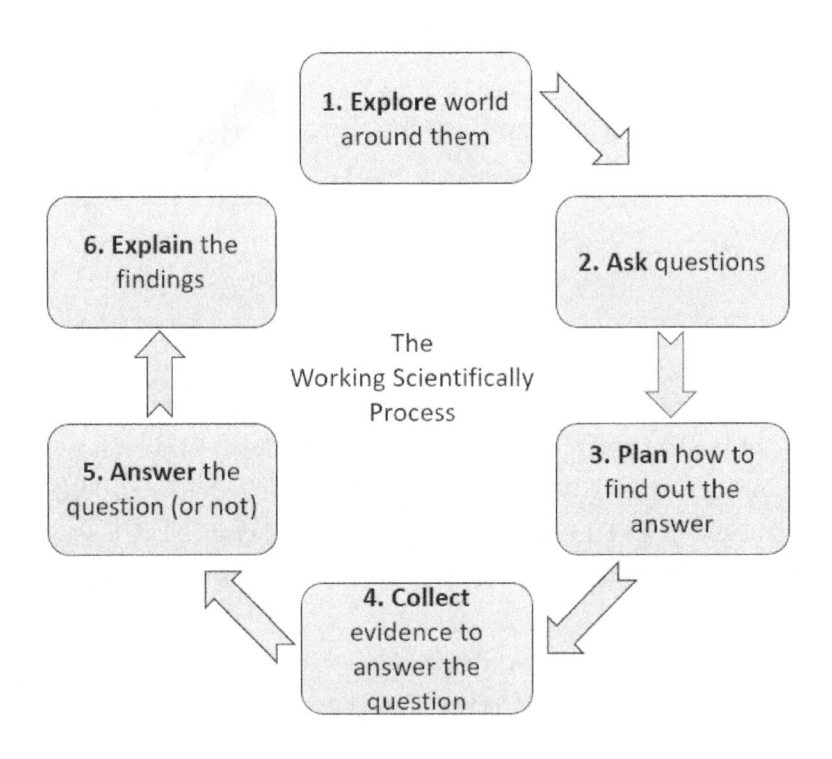

```
                    1. Explore world
                      around them

6. Explain the                          2. Ask questions
   findings
                  The
              Working Scientifically
                  Process

5. Answer the                           3. Plan how to
question (or not)                       find out the
                                            answer

                    4. Collect
                   evidence to
                   answer the
                    question
```

Do scientists know everything?

It might seem like science has an answer for everything, but there's still a lot they don't know. And even the things we know are not always completely understood. Even something as fundamental as gravity is not fully understood.

Science is about building models to explain something based on the best evidence available at the time. If new evidence can be found that suggests something different, and that evidence can be backed up and checked by others, then even long-held ideas can be updated and amended.

What is a theory?

A theory to a scientist means a different thing than it does to everyone else. In everyday use, a theory means a guess or a hunch. These theories are often unproven.

In science a theory is a well-accepted explanation for a phenomenon based on the best evidence available. A theory ties together all the facts and can be used to make predictions which can be tested. In science a theory is a close to proven as it is possible to be with the evidence available at the time. Gravity may be a "theory" but are you prepared to test it by jumping out of a window?

As well as the theory of gravity, other famous theories you should have heard of include Einstein's Theory of Relativity, Darwin's Theory of Evolution through Natural Selection and many more.

The Big Ideas in Science

So, what are the big ideas that underpin the science curriculum? What are the important concepts we need to cover?

Professor Wynne Harlen, along with a team of science experts, put together a list of scientific principles (Harlen, 2010) that underpin the science knowledge of all pupils throughout their time in school.

It was felt that the main purpose of science education is to enable every individual to take an informed part of decisions and actions that affect their own well-being and the well-being of society and the environment. Therefore, a broad understanding of science concepts is important, to have a scientifically literate population of adults.

There are 10 big ideas of science:

1. All material in the Universe is made of very small particles.
2. Objects can affect other objects at a distance.

3. Changing the movement of an object requires a net force to be acting on it.
4. The total amount of energy in the Universe is always the same but energy can be transformed when things change or are made to happen.
5. The composition of the Earth and its atmosphere and the processes occurring within them shape the Earth's surface and its climate.
6. The solar system is a very small part of one of millions of galaxies in the Universe.
7. Organisms are organised on a cellular basis.
8. Organisms require a supply of energy and materials for which they are often dependent on or in competition with other organisms.
9. Genetic information is passed down from one generation of organisms to another.
10. The diversity of organisms, living and extinct, is the result of evolution.

And also 4 Big Ideas **About** Science:

1. Science assumes that for every effect there is one or more causes
2. Scientific explanations, theories and models are those that best fit the facts known at a particular time
3. The knowledge produced by science is used in some technologies to create products to serve human ends
4. Applications of science often have ethical, social, economic and political implications

Throughout the primary national curriculum, nearly all these big ideas are introduced. The only big idea that is not covered relates to the concept of energy, and it was decided that this concept should be held back until Key Stage 3 when pupils can best understand quite an abstract idea, although some of it, such as Renewable Energy is covered in KS2 Geography instead.

Video Link: https://youtu.be/TYyoI6GYFnI

Working Scientifically Skills

What do we actually mean by "working scientifically"?

Many science curricula have some notion that pupils need to understand the nature, processes and methods of science across the key stages. These skills may be termed "Working Scientifically", "Scientific Enquiry" or similar.

Progression of Enquiry Skills

Moving from lower to upper primary, pupils should become increasingly autonomous in their decision-making when carrying out investigations. They should become systematic and accurate in collecting and analysing data; and able to express their ideas scientifically using scientific language and enquiry.

Lower KS1 Planning: Begin to think of their own ideas for experiments and say what they think will happen. Carrying Out: Make simple observations. Start to take simple measurements of things such as time, length, mass. Analysing: Draw simple charts. Attempt to link their prediction to what they found out. Were they right/wrong?
Lower KS2 Planning: Suggest questions to test and make predictions. Plan a fair and/or accurate experiment. Carrying Out: Make relevant recordings with the appropriate accuracy. Analysing: Present results in bar charts and tables. Use scientific knowledge. Decide if the evidence supports their idea. Evaluating: Explain the need to repeat some measurements for reliability.
Upper KS2 Planning: Suggest questions to test and predict using science knowledge. Plan their own experiments, decide on evidence they need to collect, and equipment needed. Carrying Out: Use a range of equipment accurately. Present results in most appropriate way. Analysing: Make comparisons using charts and graphs. Use their results to suggest further experiments to be tested. Evaluating: Identify results that do not seem to fit the pattern observed. Decide when observations need to be repeated to improve reliability.

Types of Investigation

Fair tests

In this type of enquiry, a single variable is changed while all others are kept the same. While this is a very good way to answer types of questions, it is not the only type of enquiry that can be used in the classroom.

Some studies have shown that fair testing can dominate, and over 50% of all practical activities involved a fair test–type activity. Pupils can be led to believe that only "fair" tests can be trusted.

There are many occasions when a fair test is the best method for the question being asked, such as finding out which surface is the best for stopping a runaway car at the bottom of a ramp. The size of the car, the height of the ramp and position the car is let go from should all be kept the same. Only the material at the bottom of the ramp should be changed (sand, grass, carpet, gravel etc. These are known as the variables).

Other types of investigation

As well as a fair test, there are other types of scientific enquiry activity that pupils can carry out in the classroom that may be better suited to answer different kinds of questions.

Observing over time: Taking measurements or observations over a week/month or longer. For example, "How will the seeds that we've planted change over time?" or "How long will it take for this biodegradable bag to break down if we bury it?"

Identifying and Classifying: Putting things into different groups based on observable properties. For example, "which clothes will keep us cool in the summer and which will keep us warm in the winter?" or "Put these materials into different groups based on their properties".

Pattern Seeking: Looking for patterns in sets of data. For example, "Does foot size relate to height in humans?" or "Do pupils with longer legs jump further?"

Research (using secondary sources): Using books and the internet to find out things that might be difficult to test in the classroom. For example, "how did people tell the time before clocks?"

Video Link: https://youtu.be/77Yw6pKX1oI

Things to consider

Don't always feel that every science practical has to involve the pupils in planning out a full investigation.

Do have lessons where the objective focuses on a single skill area – such as planning an experiment, collecting and recording data, presenting data or drawing conclusions. Other aspects could be decided by the teacher to speed things up.

Also think about:

- What's the learning objective
- What's the Working Scientifically objective?
- What could be your starting point?
- What questions could you ask?
- What do you want the pupils to do?
- How will they record what they do?
- What are the possible outcomes?

Ofsted says that the most effective science teachers make it a priority to maintain curiosity in their pupils (Ofsted, 2013), and making this a key principle of working scientifically by enquiry can be very beneficial (McCrory, 2017) in helping pupils see themselves as scientists.

Task: Reflect on the different types of science enquiry you have used in the past with your class. Do you only do fair testing? What other types of enquiry activity have you tried recently?

Collecting and Presenting Data

Ways of Collecting Data

Younger pupils will simply observe events rather than measure or compare them. At this level, pupils can look for changes and describe what has happened.

Older pupils may still use observations when relevant, but they should be moving more towards taking measurements using the correct units.

When working in groups, pupils could be allocated roles so that there is a "measurer" who is taking the readings and a "scribe" who is writing them down on a results sheet. Swap these roles around regularly.

Data Collecting Equipment

At a basic level, tables can be used to collect readings and observations. Older pupils could construct these themselves, but blank table scaffolds can be provided to give pupils a guide.

Digital technologies can be helpful as well: pupils could use digital cameras to take photographs or even use simple voice recorders to record their observations. If available, datalogging equipment could be used to monitor changes over long periods of time, such as temperature changes in a school pond, or light levels in the school over the course of a day.

Tablet computers can be very useful in the science classroom. They allow pupils to quickly take photographs and even videos of their experiments. Pupils can quickly add notes and labels to explain what is happening, even adding their own voiceovers.

Presenting Data

There are different ways to present their findings, depending on the type of data collected as well as the skills that have been taught in maths/numeracy lessons.

Young pupils could draw simple pictograms with assistance. Lower primary should be able to start drawing simple bar charts, they may need support choosing a suitable scale. Upper primary should be able to draw both line and scatter graphs. Some pupils may need scaffolding to help produce charts and tables and these may be presented to them partially completed, whereas other pupils would be expected to create these from scratch.

Simple spreadsheets or databases could also be set up to draw graphs based on the data inputted by the pupils. This could be a good way to collect in whole-class data to be presented on the screen at the front of the class or shared via the cloud for all pupils to then access. For example, collecting in data on the height, eye colour and hair colour of the class which they can then all access to produce graphs and charts.

Useful Links

CIEC – Working Scientifically in the Primary Classroom https://www.york.ac.uk/ciec/resources/primary/skills-for-science/

Enquiring Science4All: https://seerih-innovations.org/enquiringscience4all/

Flynn. S., (2019) Science Literacy. Science Education for Everyday Life. Chartered College https://impact.chartered.college/article/science-literacy-science-education-everyday-life/

Harlen, W. (ed). (2010) Principles and Big Ideas of Science Education. ASE. Available from: https://www.ase.org.uk/bigideas

How 'Science Capital' can help us address inequalities in STEM participation https://www.ucl.ac.uk/ioe/news/2020/may/how-science-capital-can-help-us-address-inequalities-stem-participation-rftrw-s01e03

McCrory. A., (2017) Scientific enquiry and engaging primary-aged children in science

lessons pt2. Why Teach Science via Enquiry? Journal of Emergent Science. 14. P28-39. https://www.ase.org.uk/resources/journal-of-emergent-science/issue-13

McCrory. A., (2017) Scientific enquiry and engaging primary-aged children in science lessons pt2. Why Teach Science via Enquiry? Journal of Emergent Science. 14. P28-39. https://www.ase.org.uk/resources/journal-of-emergent-science/issue-13

Ofsted (2013) Maintaining curiosity: a survey into science education in schools. https://www.gov.uk/government/publications/maintaining-curiosity-a-survey-into-science-education-in-schools

Ofsted (2013) Maintaining curiosity: a survey into science education in schools. https://www.gov.uk/government/publications/maintaining-curiosity-a-survey-into-science-education-in-schools

Primary Science Teacher Trust. Enquiry Approaches: https://pstt.org.uk/resources/curriculum-materials/enquiry-approaches

Primary Science Teacher Trust: Science Skills https://pstt.org.uk/resources/curriculum-materials/enquiry-skills

Scientific Enquiry in the UK (2018) The ASE. Available from: https://www.ase.org.uk/resources/scientific-enquiry-in-uk

Turner, J., Keogh, B., Naylor, S. and Lawrence, L. (2011) It's Not Fair (or is it). A guide to developing pupil's ideas through primary science enquiry. Millgate House.

Wellcome (2014) Primary Science, Is It Missing Out? https://cms.wellcome.org/sites/default/files/primary-science-is-it-missing-out-wellcome-sep14.pdf

12

Planning a Science Lesson

Lesson planning is something that a lot of new teachers worry about, and struggle with. There is no recipe for the perfect lesson, but successful lessons share many of the same features.

These can include:

- **Clear learning objectives:** Make the pupils aware of what they are doing, why they are doing it and what the bigger picture is. Use clear and simple language to let the pupils know what they will learn and what they will be able to do at the end.
- **A good start to the lesson:** Start the lesson with a hook to engage the pupils and get them interested in what they will be learning.
- **Lesson activities:** Match the activities to the learning outcomes. Provide a variety of activities and allow for both group and individual work. Pace the activities well so that the pupils stay engaged.
- **Differentiation:** Be aware of the range of abilities in the class, and prepare suitable tasks, scaffolding and questions where possible.
- **Review the learning:** Check what the pupils are learning throughout the lesson through mini plenaries. Summarise everything in a plenary at the end of the lesson.
- **Assessment:** Use quick assessment tasks to check that the pupils are making progress through the lesson.

These features are explained in more detail here: https://www.sciencefix.co.uk/2021/01/an-introduction-to-primary-science-lesson-planning/

Learning Objectives

Learning objectives describe what the pupils should know, understand or be able to do by the end of the lesson.

The learning objectives for a lesson should focus on two key areas of science:

- Knowledge Outcomes: Key science ideas and concepts
- Skills Outcomes: Skills related to working scientifically

Learning objectives put the lesson in context, letting the pupils understand how what they will be doing fits in with the bigger picture. Learning objectives can be displayed at the start of a lesson and explained to the pupils. They should be written in a language that is easily understood. Learning objectives can be reviewed during the plenary at the end of the lesson.

Effective learning objectives state what the pupils will learn in the lesson, rather than what they will do. For example, "To be able to explain how the phases of the moon are formed" or "Understand what a plant needs to stay healthy" are good examples of learning objectives

Read this article by James Durran about using key learning questions as an alternative to traditional learning objectives: https://jamesdurran.blog/2021/08/28/key-learning-questions-an-introduction/

Ideas for Lesson Starters

A good lesson starter should engage and motivate pupils immediately, providing a hook upon which the rest of the lesson hangs. The more engaging the hook, the more motivated the pupils will be during the remainder of the lesson.

This might include:

Mystery object: Show the pupils an object related to the lesson and ask them to come up with questions about it. Working in pairs, they can try to answer the questions, before sharing their ideas with the class.

Images: Display an image that will make the pupils think. You could zoom in or hide most of the image and ask the pupils to guess what they think it is. Gradually reveal more of the image.

Odd one out: Present the pupils with words, phrases or images and ask the pupils to identify the odd one out, justifying their answers.

Video: Show a short video clip to introduce the lesson topic. Pose an interesting question about the video and have the pupils work in pairs to try to answer it.

Websites such as Explorify (https://explorify.uk/) provide useful resources which can be great as a lesson starter to provoke questions and discussions.

Practical work

The purpose of any practical work should be clearly defined (Ofsted 2021). Is the practical work designed to support the learning of an aspect of knowledge, or is carrying it out a goal in itself? It might be that the practical activity itself is the goal – such as helping the pupils to learn how to use a thermometer or carry out another aspect of scientific enquiry.

Ofsted (2021) suggests that high-quality practical work has a clear purpose, forms part of a wider instructional sequence and takes place only when pupils have enough prior knowledge to learn from the activity.

Useful Links

Durran, J., (2021) Key Learning Questions, An Introduction https://jamesdurran.blog/2021/08/28/key-learning-questions-an-introduction/

Green, J. Lesson Planning in Science. https://thescienceteacher.co.uk/lesson-planning/

Lockyer, S., (2016) Lesson Planning for Primary School Teachers

Nicholson, D. (2021) An introduction to Primary Science Lesson Planning https://www.sciencefix.co.uk/2021/01/an-introduction-to-primary-science-lesson-planning/

Ofsted (2021) Research Review Series: Science https://www.gov.uk/government/publications/research-review-series-science/research-review-series-science

13

Structuring a Science Course

As a trainee teacher, you will not have any say in the long term, overall structure of the science course you will be teaching in your placement schools, but it is good to start to develop an understanding of how and why the course is structured in the way that it is.

"Careful curriculum design, where new knowledge is broken down into meaningful components and introduced sequentially, can support all pupils to learn scientific concepts." (Ofsted 2021)

The way that a science course is structured is the responsibility of each school. They can take their cues from the National Curriculum, but there is scope for the reordering of units, as long as it can be justified.

The way that a school structures their science course will reflect their Intent and Implementation (as outlined by Ofsted)

Intent: Consider what you want the pupils to learn, and the skills you want them to acquire. Be clear on exactly what these aims are. What do your teachers think is their objective in teaching that subject?

Implementation: How do you put your curriculum plans into practice, and how do you ensure that your intent is being carried out. How likely is it that the teaching methods used will deliver the teacher's objectives for each subject?

What do Ofsted Say?

"A high-quality science curriculum not only identifies the important concepts and procedures for pupils to learn, but it also plans for how pupils will build knowledge of these over time. This starts in the early years. Research shows that high-quality science curriculums are coherent. This means the curriculums are organised so that pupils' knowledge of concepts develops from component knowledge that is sequenced according to the logical structure of the scientific disciplines. In this way, pupils learn how knowledge connects in science as they 'see' its underlying conceptual structure. Importantly, this sequencing pays careful attention to how to pair substantive with disciplinary knowledge, so that disciplinary knowledge is always learned within the most appropriate substantive contexts." (Ofsted 2021)

As pupils progress through the science curriculum, new knowledge gets systematically integrated into pre-existing knowledge. This forms larger concepts and new ones, which in turn allow pupils to operate at more abstract levels. (Ofsted 2021)

Other factors affecting a long-term plan

There are other factors to consider when looking at how the science course is organised through a year. Units which require the pupils to go outside and look at plants and minibeasts will be difficult to teach in the winter months and so should be scheduled early in the academic year or after Easter. Sometimes consideration needs to be made for the availability of resources, so if there are parallel year 4 classes needing to cover electricity then maybe they teach the units in a slightly different order to avoid a clash. Same goes for when year 4 and year 6 are looking at electricity, or year 3 and year 6 light.

Look at your school plans for each year. How are the units organised? Do they follow the order of the National Curriculum, or have they been moved around? Are there clear links between different units.

Primary Science Route Map

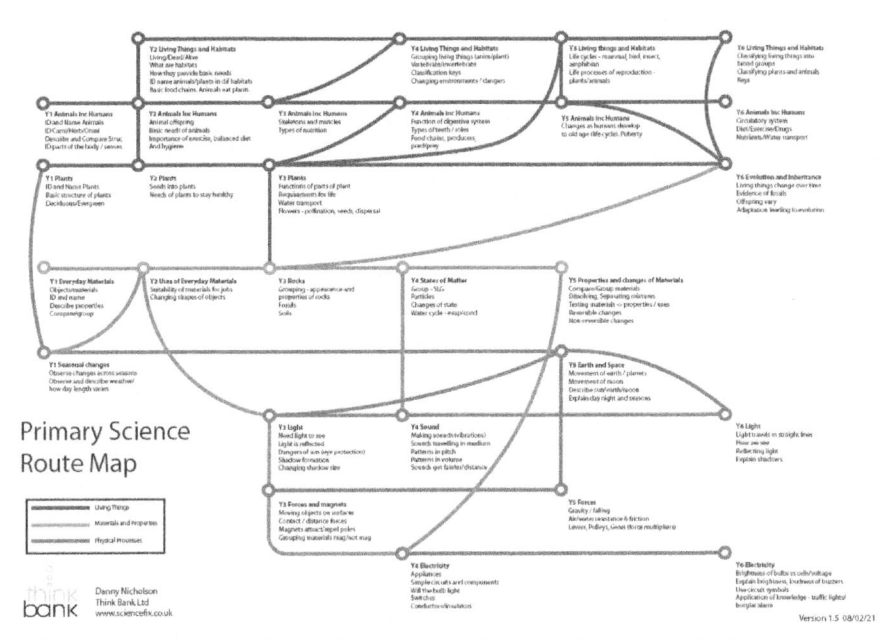

https://www.sciencefix.co.uk/2021/01/primary-science-curriculum-route-map/

Useful Links

Harlen, W. and Qualter, A. The teaching of science in primary schools, David Fulton Publishers Ltd.

Nicholson, D. (2021) Primary Science Curriculum Route Map https://www.sciencefix.co.uk/2021/01/primary-science-curriculum-route-map/

Ofsted Research Series: Science (2021) https://www.gov.uk/government/publications/research-review-series-science/research-review-series-scie nce

14

Progression of Science ideas and content

In their research review of science (2021) Ofsted describes a high quality science curriculum as something that plans for how pupils will build knowledge over time.

Early science draws on the pupil's experiences of the world around them such as local plants, their pets, their own bodies, shadows etc.

Simple explanations can be given for some phenomena, which are then revisited as the pupils get older. Not every idea can be introduced in early education, and some concepts should be introduced at a later stage, once the basics are understood.

In school science, small ideas should build and combine, gradually forming bigger ideas.

Harlen (2010 and 2015) identifies three main models of progression in ideas.

The ladder model likens progression with climbing a ladder. Each step has to be completed before the next step can be taken.

The jigsaw model describes an overall end point which can be reached in a variety of different ways in the way that a jigsaw can be completed by putting the pieces down in any order to complete the bigger picture.

The strand model breaks overall goals into several strands. Each strand develops over time, often by visiting and revisiting concepts through a spiral curriculum.

Each model has strengths and weaknesses, and the national curriculum has aspects of each in its design. The 1999 National Curriculum had might tighter spiralling, with concepts being revisited much more frequently. With the 2014 curriculum, concepts such as light or electricity only appear twice, a year or so apart.

Progression of Scientific Ideas

In their book, "The Teaching of Science in Primary Schools" Harlen and Qualter outlined several different dimensions to the progression of ideas. These are:

1. From a description to an explanation. Younger pupils may be able to describe a phenomenon, such as an object making sounds that we can hear. Older pupils will be able to offer more of an explanation, such as how sound travels as vibrations.
2. From small to big ideas. Small ideas allow the pupils to make sense of specific situations and become bigger as they are linked together into general principles that can be applied to other situations. For example, they may be to describe why an animal such as a woodlouse lives in a certain habitat. The idea becomes bigger as it becomes linked to requirements of all animals, and then all living things in general.
3. From personal to shared ideas. Young pupils look at things from their own point of view and interpret them based on this thinking. As they develop, their ideas are influenced by those of others. They understand how their learning relates to the general scientific view.

Useful Links

Harlen, W. and Qualter, A. (2018) The teaching of science in primary schools, David Fulton Publishers Ltd. Chapter 11.

Harlen, W. (ed). (2010) Principles and Big Ideas of Science Education. ASE. Available from: https://www.ase.org.uk/bigideas

Harlen, W. (ed). (2015) Working with Big Ideas of Science Education. IAP.

Available from: https://www.ase.org.uk/bigideas

Ofsted (2021) Research Review Series: Science https://www.gov.uk/government/publications/research-review-series-science/research-review-series-science

15

Taking Science Outside of the Classroom

Taking science outside of the primary classroom can provide first-hand experiences of the local environment that allow pupils to observe science taking place in the real world. This embeds their learning of science into meaningful contexts and provides opportunities for novel and exciting learning experiences.

The Natural Connections Project (2016) found it was possible for school grounds and local greenspaces to be used daily to enhance teaching and learning right across the curriculum. A 2008 Ofsted study of pupil's experiences show that first-hand experiences of learning outside the classroom help to make subjects more vivid and interesting for pupils and also enhance their understanding. It found that this can also contribute significantly to pupils' personal, social and emotional development. Learners of all ages said that they enjoyed working away from the classroom and that they found it 'exciting', 'practical', 'motivating', 'refreshing' and 'fun'.

Things to Consider

When planning to take the pupils outside, consider:

What are the learning objectives and benefits? Be clear about why learning is taking place in a particular environment (Spring 2021). Ensure you have a clear vision of what you want the activity to achieve. What do you want the pupils to experience and what skills do you want them to acquire?

How many additional staff and helpers will you need? Keep them informed of the learning objectives and how they will support the pupils.

What are the potential risks? How will you minimise them? Carry out a risk assessment before you go.

How will you help the pupils to understand how the outdoor experiences connect to the work carried out in the classroom?

What in-class activities will you carry out to follow up on the outdoor activities?

Where can you go for more help and support? There are lots of outdoor learning and field studies websites that provide information and advice. The venue you are visiting will usually be able to provide guidance on planning a safe and fun experience so do ask them if they have any teacher guides or planning checklists you can use.

See Spring (2021) for more on this.

Handy Equipment

The exact equipment you need will depend upon the nature of the activity, but there are some items that will always prove useful. These include:

- Clipboards to help observations whilst outside
- Hand lenses or magnifying glasses to study small objects in more detail
- Plastic pots with lids and clear plastic bags for collecting specimens.
- A digital camera or tablet computer for taking photographs of things that you find.
- Cleansing wipes and hand sanitizer gel

Using the School Grounds

The areas around the school provide a rich, easy-to-access, learning resource. They offer excellent opportunities for learning, for instance...

- School playing field
- Playground
- Paths into and around the school
- School buildings and walls.

Consider the facilities available to you at your school. Is there a school nature area or school garden that can be used? Does the school have a pond?

If the school does not have a nature area or garden, could a class project be to set one up? Perhaps the pupils could design a place for insects to live or a small flowerbed to attract pollinating insects like bees and butterflies.

Taking Messy Things Outside

Sometimes, going outside makes certain activities easier to deal with, especially if there is a risk of mess or a lot of space is needed. This includes:

- Planting bulbs and seeds
- activities using water such as floating and sinking
- looking at how heart rate changes with exercise
- modelling the solar system

I once observed a lesson on sound where the pupils looked at how a drum skin vibrates by putting bird seed on it. This took place on the playground, and at the end of the lesson, the seeds were left for the birds to eat instead of making a mess in the classroom!

Useful Links

Grimshaw, M., Curwen, L., Morgan, J., Shallcross, N., Franklin, S., and Shallcross, D., (2019) The Benefits of Outdoor Learning on Science Teaching. Journal of Emergent Science. 16: 40:45 https://www.ase.org.uk/system/files/Grimshaw%20et%20al_0.pdf

Natural Connections Demonstration Project (2016) Transforming Outdoor

Learning in Schools-Lessons https://www.plymouth.ac.uk/uploads/production/document/path/7/7634/Transforming_Outdoor_Learning_in_Schools_SCN.pdf

Nicholson, D., (2020) Teaching Primary Science Outside of the Classroom https://www.sciencefix.co.uk/2020/06/teaching-primary-science-outside-of-the-classroom/

Ofsted (2008) Learning Outside the Classroom https://www.lotc.org.uk/wp-content/uploads/2010/12/Ofsted-Report-Oct-2008.pdf

Spring, H., (2021) Why Choose to Learn Outside? Journal of Emergent Science 21 p23-29 https://www.ase.org.uk/resources/journal-of-emergent-science/issue-21

Woodland Trust Outdoor Learning Pack https://www.woodlandtrust.org.uk/media/43645/outdoor-learning-resource-pack.pdf

16

Dealing with Science Misconceptions

Pupils do not come into school as an empty vessel, ready to be filled with science knowledge, rather they come with their own sets of ideas and concepts that they will have built to explain how the world around them works. This is a *constructivist* view of learning, drawing on the work of psychologists such as Piaget and Vygotsky. Leinhardt (1992) stated that the essence of constructivist theory is the idea that learners must individually discover and transform complex information if they are to make it their own.

Often these existing ideas are produced through informal play or through watching films and television shows. These ideas are at odds with the accepted science, and they can be difficult to change or reform and become a source of misconceptions when met in formal science lessons (Allen, 2010). Misconceptions can represent a barrier to learning.

Strategies for Eliciting Misconceptions

Before a misconception can be corrected, they need to be identified. There are many different strategies a teacher can use to find out what misconceptions pupils have. These ideas can include:

Questioning: The most straightforward way is to ask the pupils directly and elicit their ideas in this way. This could be combined with mini-whiteboards where all pupils can write their answer then hold it up. Diagnostic Question

Banks can also be used.

Concept cartoons: Brenda Keogh and Stuart Naylor pioneered the use of concept cartoons in the early 90's to promote discussion and elicit and challenge pupil's ideas. Concept cartoons are used to present a scientific concept within an everyday situation which a group of cartoon pupils are discussing. Different viewpoints are shown, which the pupils might agree or disagree with, revealing any misconceptions. For more, see Naylor and Keogh (2012).

Drawings: Asking the pupils to draw or annotate a picture can give the teacher an idea of what the pupils are thinking. For example, if asked to draw different animals do the pupils only draw four legged animals, or do they include snakes/fish/birds etc. (Allen 2012). These diagrams can be used as a basis for further questions.

Concept maps: There are different ways to create concept maps. A simple way is for the teacher to provide all the key words for the pupils to cut out. Associated words are stuck down and linked with pencil lines. Each line is accompanied by a comment explaining why they are linked (Allen 2019)

For more ideas for eliciting misconceptions, see Allen (2019)

Dealing with Misconceptions

So how do you correct a misconception when you've found out what they are?

The challenge for a primary teacher is to organise the child's naive ideas and misconceptions into coherent concepts which are accurate and explicit. These misconceptions cannot be ignored since they are the foundations upon which new knowledge is built. (Pine 2001).

Link any intervention with the prior knowledge. Introduce a situation where the misconception is shown – such as a clip from a movie showing loud explosions in space before discussing that sound cannot travel in a vacuum.

Investigating the concept through practical work can also help address the misconception. Pupils can make their prediction – what they think will happen and why they think that. They can then see if their prediction is correct. If their prediction is shown to be wrong, this can result in cognitive conflict. The pupil will then hopefully reject their wrong idea and assimilate the scientific concept.

Although this relates to making science videos, this video by Derek Muller of Veritasium explains the process of addressing misconceptions which can be adapted into science lessons: https://youtu.be/RQaW2bFieo8

For a comprehensive approach to dealing with a wide range of science misconceptions, then I highly recommend getting hold of a copy of Allen (2019)

To do: Read this Monarch and Turford (2012) article about dealing with misconceptions related to levers, pulleys and gears. (link https://pstt.org.uk/application/files/1115/5196/9591/Spring_2019_common_misconceptions.pdf) Think about a common science misconception the pupils might have in relation to a topic you are teaching at the moment. How might you address this misconception, and help pupils understand what is really happening?

Useful Links

Allen, M., (2019) Misconceptions in Primary Science. Open University Press.

Monach, J., Turford, B., (2019) Common Misconceptions. Levers, Gears and Pulleys. Primary Science Teaching Trust https://pstt.org.uk/application/files/1115/5196/9591/Spring_2019_common_misconceptions.pdf

Muller, D., (2012) The key to effective educational science videos https://youtu.be/RQaW2bFieo8

Nicholson, D. (2021). Addressing Misconceptions in Primary Science https://www.sciencefix.co.uk/2021/12/addressing-misconceptions-in-primary-science/

Pine, K., Messer, D., & St. John, K., (2001) Pupils Misconceptions in Primary Science: A Survey of teachers' views, Research in Science & Technological Education,

19:1, 79-9 https://doi.org/10.1080/02635140120046240

17

Questioning in Primary Science

Questioning is an integral part of the teaching process, particularly in science. So how do you ask the right questions? In this section we'll explore that.

It's said that teachers ask nearly 400 questions a day (ASCD, 2008). Questioning enables teachers to check pupils' understanding at key points in the lesson. It also encourages engagement and focuses the pupils' thinking on key concepts and ideas. The kinds of questions that teachers ask, and the way teachers ask these questions can, to some extent, influence the type of cognitive processes that pupils engage in as they grapple with the process of constructing scientific knowledge (Chin, 2007).

Questions can be used at the start of a lesson to find out the pupils' ideas and what they already know about a particular topic. This can help to identify misconceptions. Every investigation should begin with a question or a problem that can be answered through exploration. Questions can be used in a plenary to stimulate pupils to reflect on their experiences in the lesson.

Teachers can use questions in different ways:

- Questions for finding out pupils' ideas: "What do you think is happening…?"
- Questions for encouraging predictions: "What do you think will happen if…?"
- Questions to encourage planning: "How will you make this a fair test?"

- Questions to encourage further questions: "What other things would you like to know about rainforests?"

Wonder Walls

Effective questioning should not be a one-way process. Pupils should be encouraged to ask more questions. Start by asking "What things would you like to know about this topic?" In this way they could generate their own questions for research or for investigation. You might use a **KWL** grid to let pupils record what they **Know**, what they **Want** to know and what they have **Learnt**.

Taking this idea further, some teachers set up a "Wonder Wall" on a display board in their classroom for pupils to post the questions they have at the start of a unit of work, and they can add to it as the unit progresses. See this blog post for more: https://www.madlylearning.com/wonderwall/

Open and closed questions

Closed questions are often used to evaluate what pupils know. The teacher asks a closed question that is basically information-seeking, that requires a predetermined short answer, and that is usually pitched at the recall or lower-order cognitive level (Chin, 2007).

Closed questions can be answered with either a short word or phrase, or can be answered with just a simple yes or no. Closed questions are good for giving you facts. They are easy and quick to answer.

Closed questions can be useful as opening questions since they are easy for the pupils to answer. They could be used for quick fire questions around a particular topic area. But they do not allow the pupils much room to explain what they think. They mainly deal with recall questions.

Examples of closed questions

- Is ice a solid?

- Did the cress seeds germinate when water was added?
- Which parachute fell the slowest, the large one or the small one?

In comparison, **open questions** allow the pupils to give a long answer. They give the pupils a chance to think and reflect (Chin, 2007). Questioning is used to diagnose and extend pupils ideas and to scaffold pupils thinking. Open questions begin with words such as what, how, why, describe, predict. They can allow for higher order thinking.

Examples of open questions

- What properties does ice have that made you classify it as a solid?
- Describe what conditions are needed for cress seeds to germinate?
- How did the size of the parachute affect the speed that it falls?

Blooms Taxonomy and Questions

Questioning enables teachers to check pupils' understanding at key points in the lesson. It also encourages engagement and focuses the pupils' thinking on key concepts and ideas.

Bloom's Taxonomy is one approach that can be used to help plan and formulate higher order questions. It arranges questions based on their level of complexity, from basic knowledge and understanding of a concept or process to higher levels of critical and creative thinking.

Evaluation

Synthesis

Analysis

Application

Comprehension

Knowledge

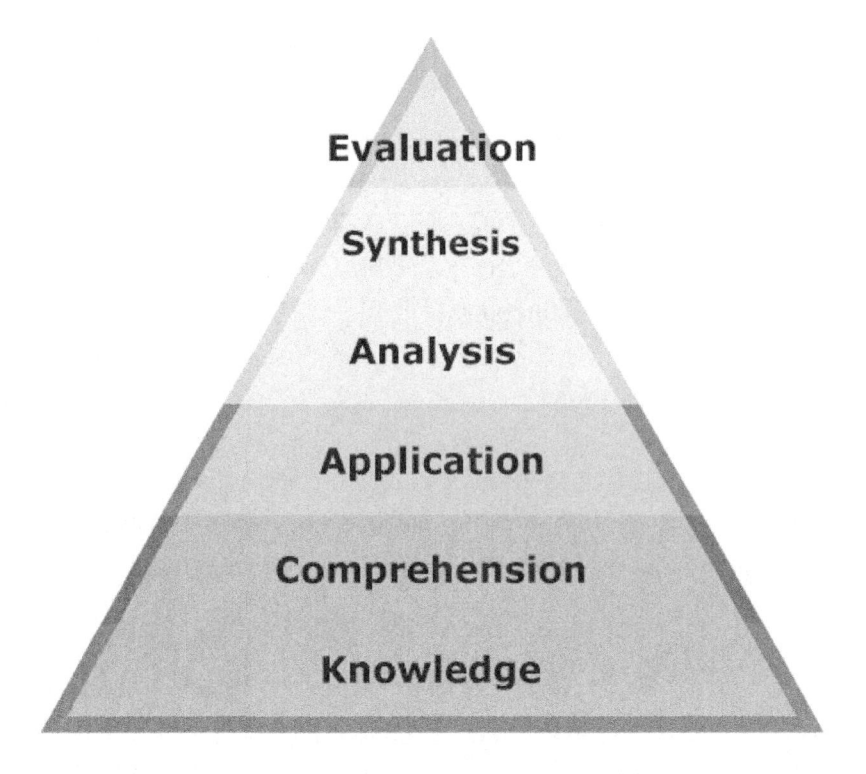

https://commons.wikimedia.org/wiki/File:Bloom_taxonomy.jpg

Basic Recall: Knowledge: What, when, who, identify

Demonstrating Understanding: Comprehension: Compare, predict, explain, contrast.

Using Knowledge: Application: Build, plan, how would, test.

Examining Information: Analysis: Why did this happen? What would have happened if...?

Creating something new: Synthesis: Could you design...? How might you stop X happening?

Assessing value: Evaluation: Is there a better way to do? Is this a good or bad thing?

Keep this hierarchy in mind when planning the progression of questions to use. You might start with some simple knowledge questions, then move up to higher order questioning.

Questioning techniques

Instead of asking a question and waiting for hands up, some different questioning techniques to try include:

- Turn to your neighbour – pupils discuss the question with a someone sitting nearby.
- Think-pair-share: first think individually, then discuss with a partner and then share their thinking with the class.
- Cold calling: ask the question then choose a child to answer instead of hands up. Can use lollipop sticks to select a child at random.
- Mini Whiteboards: pupils use individual whiteboards to write down their answers and then show the class or group.

Useful Links

ASCD (2008) Asking Good Questions https://www.ascd.org/el/articles/asking-good-questions

Chin, C., (2007) Teacher Questioning in Science Classrooms: Approaches that Stimulate Productive Thinking. Journal of Research in Science Teaching. 44.6 pp815-843 – Online at https://www.stem.org.uk/system/files/community-resources/legacy_files_migrated/10174-Chin-2007-Journal_of_Research_in_Science_Teaching.pdf

Harlen, W. (2006) Teaching Learning and Assessing Science 5-12. (Sage)

National Association for Able Pupils in Education (2019) 10 Ideas for Improve your use of questioning in science https://www.nace.co.uk/blogpost/1761881/327881/10-ideas-to-improve-your-use-of-questioning-in-science

Whitby, V. (2006) Teacher Questioning in Primary Science. Early Child Development and Care, 83:1, 109-114. https://doi.org/10.1080/0300443920830110

18

Pupil Talk in Primary Science

Pupil's talk provides them with a way to develop and express their ideas, as well as comparing them with the ideas of others, which helps to develop critical thinking.

Right across the curriculum, talk engages pupils, motivates them to use their speaking and listening skills and helps them learn how to respect and respond to each other (RSC, 2015). It reinforces the idea that mistakes can be opportunities for learning, leading pupils to find their own answers to problems. In science especially, exploratory talk helps pupils develop their enquiry and reasoning skills.

Pupil to Pupil Talk

Talking in science helps pupils to make sense of what we want them to learn. It helps them to develop an ability to reason scientifically.

Working in groups or pairs provides opportunities for the pupils to participate in discussion activities, which encourages cognitive processes that allow pupils to refine their own thinking.

A major challenge for teachers is to guide pupils towards talk that develops their understanding without dominating discussions. One strategy is for teachers to position themselves as fellow learners when intervening in group discussions. Teachers can also guide through example, by modelling the kinds of talk that they are aiming for in group work in their interactions with the pupils – offering ideas, listening to others, asking for clarification and so on.

In successful pupil–pupil discussion, all members of a group contribute, and all opinions and ideas are respected.

Pupil to Teacher Talk

The ways that teachers talk to pupils can take different forms at different parts of the lesson. Research found that science teachers needed to use different kinds of talk to enable pupils to move from their existing everyday understanding of natural phenomena towards a scientific view (see CUREE, 2011 http://www.curee.co.uk/node/4836). These included 'dialogic' episodes when teachers probed pupils' everyday ideas and 'authoritative' episodes when the teacher introduced scientific ideas. Sometimes the talk was interactive and sometimes it was not.

Dialogic talk involves exploring answers from pupils by asking for more detail or asking others in the class whether they agree or disagree.

Authoritative talk is where teachers keep the focus on the science points being addressed rather than addressing the pupils' own ideas.

Examples of dialogic talk:

- That's interesting – what do you mean by that?
- Do you agree with what Amy has just said?
- Could you explain more about what you just said?

Teacher talk can also be classified as either **interactive** or **non-interactive**. Interactive talk allows for the participation of both the teacher and the pupils, such as a question-and-answer session. Non-interactive talk is where only the teacher is talking.

	Interactive	Non-interactive
Dialogic	Teacher and pupils explore ideas and pose questions. They offer, listen to and work on different views.	Teacher considers various points of view. They set out, explore and work on different perspectives.
Authoritative	Teacher leads the pupils through sequence of questions and answers with the aim of reaching one specific point of view.	Only the teacher talks. Teacher presents one specific view.

The type of talk will depend very much on the aim of the lesson. Good teaching will move between each of these types of teaching during a lesson, opening up a subject for discussion, helping pupils to understand science concepts, summarising the science and then linking it to the pupils' own experiences.

Questions are important within science lessons. Diagnostic questions can be used to help the teacher monitor levels of understanding and to identify possible misconceptions.

For more on this, read Effective Classroom Talk in Science, by CUREE. http://www.curee.co.uk/node/4836

Strategies for Encouraging Talk

The Primary Science Teacher Trust has some excellent resources for encouraging Pupil Talk in Science as part of what they call "Bright Ideas Time", short 10 minute activities to use at any point in a lesson. This includes things like Odd One Out, PMI and Big Questions activities. Take a look at https://pstt.org.uk/resources/curriculum-materials/bright-ideas

Odd One Out: Pupils are shown 3 or 4 different pictures (or real objects if possible) and given a couple of minutes thinking time. Then they are asked to say which is the odd one out and why. The 'why' is key – the pupils justify their reasoning and so reveal their thinking. There's usually no one correct answer, anyone could be chosen as long as the reasoning is valid.

An example is given below. Which of these items would you choose?

PMI (Plus, Minus, Interesting): The pupils are given a scenario or a statement and then consider the positives, the minuses and the interesting associated ideas. For example, what if nothing decayed? What if all sounds had the same pitch?

Big Questions: Give the pupils a chance to discuss something big. Prompt with a picture, an object or a simple demonstration of a process to engage the pupils and to support your question. Why don't birds get electrocuted on power lines? Do aliens exist? etc.

Concept Cartoons: These can be used as a means of stimulating pupil discussion. Pupils can discuss the statements, and then give their own explanations.

Talking Points: These are statements about a topic that can be either factually accurate, open to debate or simply wrong. Pupils decide in pairs whether the statements are true or false. Talking points are best used in a classroom where pupils know that there are ground rules that allow for and encourage extended responses and tentative exploratory contributions.

Pictures for Talk: A powerful image can be a good stimulus to encourage pupils to engage in effective talk in science. They can also be used as a starting point for inquiry. This resource from PSTT has some useful images to get you started https://pstt.org.uk/resources/curriculum-materials/Pictures-for-Talk

As mentioned in the last section, the Explorify website is a good source of odd one out activities, PMI situations and big questions you could use. https://explorify.uk

To do: Watch the video showing pupils using concept cartoons at https://youtu.be/9GdZfpT6BVw. How is the concept cartoon stimulating pupil talk? How could you use concept cartoons in your lessons?

Useful Links

Centre for the Use of Research and Evidence in Education (CUREE). (2011) Effective Classroom Talk in Science. Pdf available from http://www.curee.co.uk/node/4836

Centre for the Use of Research and Evidence in Education (CUREE) (2001) Classroom Talk and Questioning in Science http://www.curee.co.uk/files/RMHolyRosary/Resources/Classroom_talk_and_questioning_in_science.pdf

Concept Cartoon Ideas https://explorify.uk/teaching-support/teaching-science/materials-explore-with-your-class

Nicholson, D. (2021) Encouraging Discussion and Managing Pupil Talk in Science. https://www.sciencefix.co.uk/2021/01/pupil-talk-in-science/

Primary Science Teaching Trust. Bright Ideas https://pstt.org.uk/resources/curriculum-materials/bright-ideas

Primary Science Teaching Trust: Play Observe and Ask in EYFS https://pstt.org.uk/resources/curriculum-materials/eyfs-science

Royal Society of Chemistry (2015). Talk for Primary Science https://edu.rsc.org/primary-science/talk-for-primary-science/2104.article

19

Assessment in Primary Science

Assessment is at the heart of teaching and learning. It allows teachers to make informed decisions about the needs of our learners in order to make further progress. There are two main types of assessment: formative and summative.

Formative assessment: Runs alongside the learning and informs the teacher and the children about next steps.

Summative assessment: Takes place at the end of a block of learning and sums up where learners have got to, in relation to agreed benchmarks. Usually this takes the form of an end of unit quiz or test.

Purpose of Assessment

According to Sharp et al (2014) The main functions of assessment are:

- To inform planning for future teaching
- To inform pupils about their own learning and progress and involve them in the process of assessment
- To inform subsequent teachers and the school about the pupils learning, progress, and attainment.
- To inform parents about their children's learning and progress.

Formative Assessment

Formative assessment, sometimes called Assessment for Learning (AFL), runs alongside the learning and informs the teacher and the children about next steps. It is ongoing and a regular part of the teacher's role. Formative assessment is an essential component of classroom work, and its development can raise standards of achievement (Black and William, 1998).

It allows teachers to determine their children's needs and their current level of understanding. This can allow teachers to make an informed choice. It might inform future planning, giving teachers a guide for how to adapt the next activity to build on a learners current understanding or skill level.

Black and Harrison (2004) listed four main principles in the assessment of science. These are:

- Teachers must start from where the learners are.
- Learning has to be done by the learners and not done for them
- In order to learn the learners must understand the learning targets
- Learners need to talk about their learning and reflect upon it.

The climate in the classroom is very important AFL will flourish best when pupils feel confident and safe in the classroom. They feel comfortable about sharing their ideas without ridicule or embarrassment (Hodgson 2010).

Assessment as Learning

Assessment as learning draws on the cognitive principle that pupils are more likely to remember knowledge if they practise retrieving that knowledge over extended periods of time. It involves pupils recalling information successfully from long-term memory into their working memory. (Ofsted 201)

Retrieval practice refers to the act of recalling learned information from memory, and in doing so the memory is made stronger (Jones, 2019). Younger children benefit from a more guided retrieval practice tasks, for example adding knowledge to a partially completed concept map (Ofsted 2021).

See Jones (2019) for more on retrieval practice as a strategy in the classroom.

Supporting Assessment in Primary Science

There are various guides you can refer to that will support assessment in your science lessons. Here are a few you get you started.

Teacher Assessment in Primary Science: https://pstt.org.uk/resources/curriculum-materials/assessment

CIEC Enabling Accurate Teacher Assessment in Primary Science: https://www.york.ac.uk/ciec/resources/primary/enabling-accurate-teacher-assessment/

PLAN Assessment: https://www.planassessment.com/

Formative Assessment Techniques

We've already looked at many of the assessment techniques as part of other units in this booklet, such as concept cartoons, labelling diagrams etc. Such as:

Lesson Starter Techniques
Questioning
Pupil Talk
Eliciting Misconceptions

Self-Assessment

Self-assessment has an essential role to play (Dylan and Harrison, 2004). To be successful the children should know what the desired goals for particular activities are. The learning intentions and outcomes should be clearly stated. Children can identify where they are in relation to these goals and understand how they can take steps to achieve them.

There are many different quick self-assessment techniques that can be employed through the course of a lesson to allow immediate feedback. The teacher can quickly see how well the class as a whole understands a concept, and who needs additional help. These can be linked to the learning objectives and success criteria.

Quick self-assessment techniques can include:

Whiteboards: All the children have a mini-whiteboard and pen on their table. When asked by the teacher they can rank their understanding on a scale of 1 to 3 or draw smiley or sad faces. They can write their number on the whiteboard and hold it up for the teacher to see.

Traffic Lights: The children can rate their understanding on a coloured scale. Give students red, amber and green cards to show when asked, or they could label their work with a colour. Green meant that they totally understand, amber meant they had partial understanding, and red meant they don't understand and need more help.

Thumbs up: The children can put their hands in the air when asked by the teacher. A thumbs-up gesture means they understand. Thumbs down means they need more help. A sideways thumb means they partially understand.

Peer Assessment

Peer assessment builds on the notion of learning as a co-constructivist activity where learning occurs as a result of social interaction. Children can take ownership of their learning and see it as a process in which they are involved and can make a contribution.

In pairs, children can mark each other's work. They can assess it against specific criteria, ideally agreed between themselves or as a class. Children are able to demonstrate their own understanding through assessment comments they give on their partner's work.

See Dylan and Harrison (2004) for more on this.

The TAPs Project

The Teacher Assessment in Primary Science Project (TAPS) has put together a very useful bank of resources which supports teachers and schools in developing their assessment systems. It covers formative and summative assessment, monitoring of pupil progress and whole-school reporting. It's an excellent resource for all primary teachers to take a look at. https://pstt.org.uk/resources/curriculum-materials/assessment

Useful Links

Black, P. and Harrison, C., (2004) Science Inside the Black Box. Assessment for Learning in the Science Classroom. GL Assessment. http://www.btsa.uk/library/files/Science-inside-the-black-box.pdf

Black, P., & William, D. (2010). Inside the Black Box Raising Standards Through Classroom Assessment. https://www.researchgate.net/publication/44836144_Inside_the_Black_Box_Raising_Standards_Through_Classroom_Assessment

Harlen, W., (2006). Teaching Learning and Assessing Science 5-12. (Sage)

Hodgson, C., (2010) Assessment for Learning in Primary Science: Practices and Benefits. National Foundation for Educational Research. https://www.nfer.ac.uk/publications/AAS02/AAS02.pdf

Jones, K. (2019) Retrieval Practice. Research and Resources for Every Classroom. John Catt.

Ofsted Research Series: Science (2021) https://www.gov.uk/government/publications/research-review-series-science/research-review-series-science#assessment

PLAN Assessment: https://www.planassessment.com/

Teacher Assessment in Primary Science. Primary Science Teacher Trust. https://pstt.org.uk/resources/curriculum-materials/assessment

Sharp, J., Peacock, G., Johnsey, G., Simon, S., and Smith., R., (2014) Primary Science: Teaching Theory and Practice (Achieving QTS Series). Learning

Matters. Ch8.

20

Science and Computing/ICT

Presenting Science and ICT ("Digital Storytelling")

Put simply, "digital storytelling" is just using computer-based tools to tell a story. There are many different ways to do this – from making movies, recording voices, creating animations or electronic books.

In science, technology can help to take a mundane task – such as writing a report, explaining a process or describing an experiment – and allow the pupils to demonstrate their understanding in more creative ways.

Can you use technology to do more than "just go write it up"? Can they tell a story about their experiment and what they found out?

For example, pupils can create:
- Comic strips
- E-books
- Photo slideshows
- Slide Presentations
- Flyers and leaflets
- Stop-motion animations
- Short films
- Podcasts and audio recordings

This blogpost suggests some apps to use: https://www.whiteboardblog.co.uk/2021/10/creative-tools-for-digital-storytelling-in-the-classroom/

Comics and Comic Strips

Make a comic strip to explain the results of an experiment using tools such as StoryboardThat https://www.storyboardthat.com/storyboard-creator

Audio and Video

Digital cameras are now relatively inexpensive and simple to use, and tablets such as iPads also have the ability to record video and audio. Audio recordings can also be made easily on a laptop using software such as Audacity and a cheap microphone.

Pupils can record videos of practical work and provide a commentary as they go along. Playing back videos allows the pupils to review and evaluate their work. Audio and video files could be shared on the school website or social media channels (if parent permission given).

Some cameras have the ability to make time-lapse videos, which could allow pupils to make videos of, for example, a plant growing in the classroom or a shadow moving over the course of a day.

The pupils could film their own news report about the results of an investigation, with one child as the interviewer and the other as a scientist. They could make a short documentary about the life of a famous scientist such as Mary Anning or Charles Darwin, or they could create short commercials. With a plain green bed sheet pinned to the wall some iPad apps allow for chromakey to replace the background, turning the classroom into a news studio, a rainforest or even the moon!

These can be a great way to allow the pupils to develop their communication and literacy skills. They will need to work together to create scripts, record each other and edit a finished product.

Ideas for audio or video recording include:
- Pretend to interview a famous scientist
- Describe a science investigation and its results
- Make a news report from a faraway location
- Produce a radio commercial
- "Public information" films
- Discuss a science story that has been in the news
- Read out science poems or stories written in class, perhaps adding sound effects
- Make an animation to explain a process such as a life cycle or the water cycle

Remember, the technology should be used in the classroom when it is appropriate, not just for the sake of it. It should enhance the teaching of science in the lesson, rather than being a distraction. The teacher should decide when, and when not, to use the technology.

Data Handling and ICT

Technology can support science in schools by helping pupils observe, measure, record, manipulate and interpret results. Data-logging equipment can aid the collection of data, which can then be turned into a graph and/or analysed in a spreadsheet.

Pupils' investigations in science can generate plenty of data that needs to be sorted and analysed (Kelly and Stead 2013). Software such as data loggers or spreadsheets can be used to quickly create graphs, removing the need to draw them by hand. This can free up more time for analysis. However, such software shouldn't be used every time: it is important that pupils also have

SCIENCE AND COMPUTING/ICT

the opportunity to practise drawing graphs by hand.

Pupils are expected to be able to create and use pictograms, bar charts, line graphs and scatter graphs. Data for all of these graphs can be produced during science practical work, via experiments, surveys or research. Simple formulae can be used to calculate totals and averages.

	A	B	C	D
1	Height of drop / cm	Width of Crater / cm		
2		Drop 1	Drop 2	Average
3	20	6	6	6
4	40	7	7.5	7.25
5	60	7.5	8	7.75
6	80	8	8.2	8.1
7	100	8	8.5	8.25

Colour of Eyes

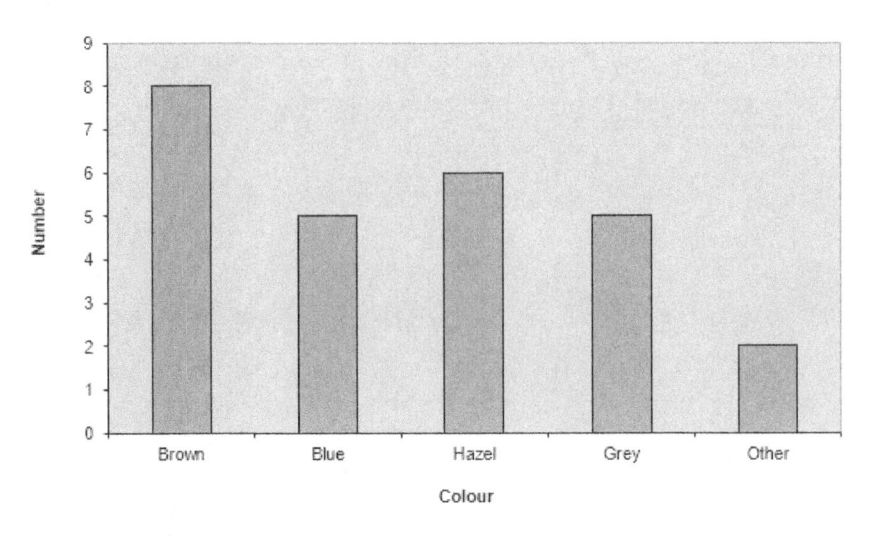

Colour	Number
Brown	8
Blue	5
Hazel	6
Grey	5
Other	2

Data Logging

Data logging provides quicker and more accurate data collection, as well as allowing you to monitor changes over long periods of time. To carry out data logging you need a computer, an interface that communicates with the computer, and sensors that communicate with the interface. You will also need special software be able to make sense of the information and display it on the screen.

Sometimes, a data-logging interface will have its own screen displaying readings from the sensors so that it can be used without having to be connected to a computer. It can then be connected to a computer to download the data.

There are many different kinds of sensors available. Temperature and light-level sensors are the most commonly used, so they good choices for your first sensors. Other sensors, such as humidity and sound sensors, can also be very useful in primary science.

SCIENCE AND COMPUTING/ICT

Two temperature probes could be used to explore why animals have fur – fill plastic cups with warm water and wrap one in cotton wool and leave one bare. Leave for 20 minutes and look at how quickly they cool.

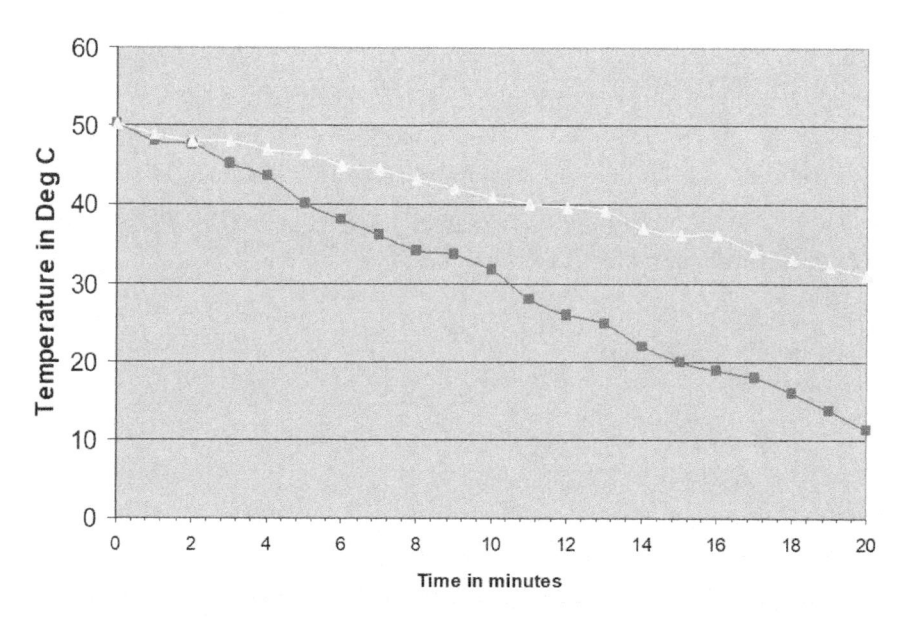

Who's the warmest? — Naked Animal / Furry Animal

A sound sensor could be used to look at sound insulation. Put a sound sensor inside a box and a noise source such as a loud alarm clock outside the box. Wrap the box in different materials to see which is best at insulating the sensor from the noise.

For a list of datalogging ideas, take a look here: https://www.sciencefix.co.uk/2019/10/datalogging-in-primary-science-a-quick-starter-guide/

Simulations

A computer simulation is an on-screen representation of a situation or a process, such as the particles in a material or an electrical circuit. Computer simulations can be a valuable tool for teaching science.

Simulations and models allow pupils to investigate abstract ideas or carry out practical work that would be difficult or time consuming in the classroom – for example, building electric circuits or looking at the motion of the planets (Massie and Long, 2009) They are also very useful for carrying out practical work as part of home learning.

Always make sure that pupils are supported in their use of simulations. Podolefsky et al. (2010) found that scaffolding is essential to support pupil engagement in science simulations. Such as ensuring the pupils are prepared with some level of understanding of the topic or basic vocabulary before embarking on the simulation. Young pupils in particular will need guidance in their use and a clear focus.

Examples of Simulations

Phet Simulations

The Phet site is an excellent resource full of simulations for all ages and subject areas. A great example of these is the circuit construction kit. This allows pupils to build and explore electrical circuits. Where possible, allow the pupils to explore a "real" circuit first, before exploring the simulation.

Unlike in the classroom there are no limitations on equipment, or safety issues, so if the pupils want to know what happens if they use 10 batteries then they can find out! (Try it out, see what happens!)

https://phet.colorado.edu/en/simulations/circuit-construction-kit-dc-virtual-lab

SCIENCE AND COMPUTING/ICT

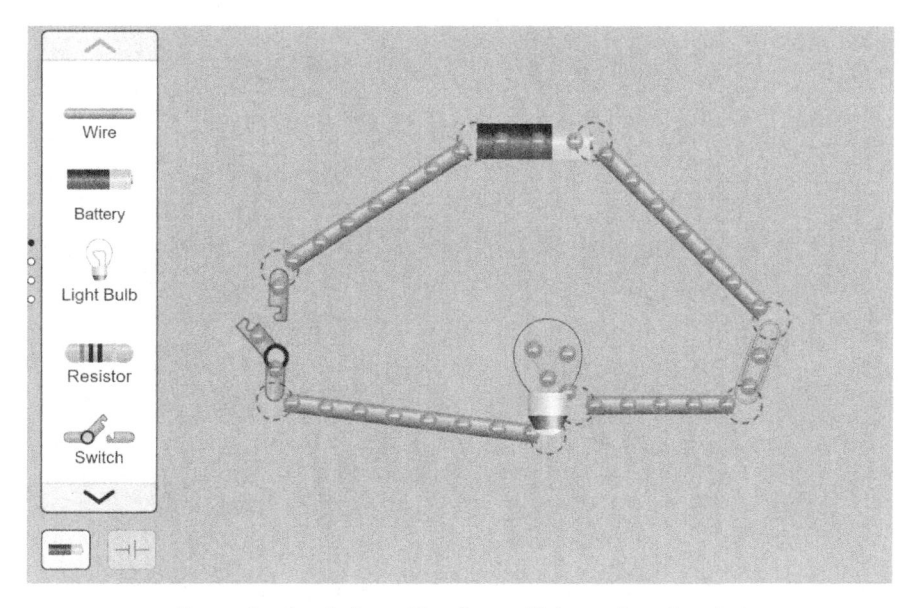

Example circuit from Phet https://phet.colorado.edu/

Solar System Scope

Solar System Scope (https://www.solarsystemscope.com/) is an online orrery, providing a simulation of the motion of the planets around the Sun. You can play the simulation forwards or backwards at different speeds to see how the planets move, or you can drag a specific planet around. You could zoom in on the inner planets or zoom right out to see how the outer planets move.

Scaffold this with a question sheet for the pupils to give them specific things to find out, such as the length of a year on different planets.

For example – a good time to send a space probe to Mars will be December 2022, when Mars is close to the Earth. By dragging Mars around the Sun to travel forward in time, could the pupils find out the next best time to send a probe to Mars? And the next?

Clicking on particular planets will bring up more information about each one along with a close-up view of the planet and its moons.

Screen shot from solar system scope https://www.solarsystemscope.com/

Useful Links

Harlen, W., and Qualter, A., (2018) The Teaching of Science in Primary Schools. Routledge

Kelly, L., and Stead, D., (2013) Enhancing Primary Science. Developing Effective Cross-Curricular Links. OUP.

Lewin, C., Smith, A., Morris, S., and Craig, E., (2019) Using Digital Technology to Improve Learning: Evidence Review. Education Endowment Foundation https://educationendowmentfoundation.org.uk/education-evidence/evidence-reviews/digital-technology-2019

Massie, J., and Long., (2009) Simulation for Science Education. Online: http://etec.ctlt.ubc.ca/510wiki/Simulation_for_Science_Education

Nicholson, D., (2019) Data Logging in Primary Science: A quick starter guide https://www.sciencefix.co.uk/2019/10/datalogging-in-primary-science-a-quick-starter-guide/

National Centre for Computing Education. What is a Spreadsheet? https://teachcomputing.org/curriculum/key-stage-2/data-and-information-spre

adsheets/lesson-1-what-is-a-spreadsheet

National Centre for Computing Education. Datalogging https://teachcomputing.org/curriculum/key-stage-2/data-and-information-data-logging

Nicholson, D. (2021) Creative Tools for Digital Storytelling in Class https://www.whiteboardblog.co.uk/2021/10/creative-tools-for-digital-storytelling-in-the-classroom/

Nicholson, D., (2016) Creative Use of ICT In Science https://www.whiteboardblog.co.uk/2016/01/creative-use-of-ict-in-science-ase-talk-2016/

Phet Simulations https://phet.colorado.edu/

Podolefsky, N., Perkins, K. and Adams, W. (2010) Factors Promoting Engaged Exploration with Computer Simulations Phys. Rev. ST Phys. Educ. Res. 6 https://journals.aps.org/prper/abstract/10.1103/PhysRevSTPER.6.020117

Storyboard that: https://www.storyboardthat.com/storyboard-creator

Solar System Scope: https://www.solarsystemscope.com/

21

Raising Interest and Challenging Stereotypes in Science

Scientists and Stereotypes

Have you ever searched the Internet for an image of a scientist? If you haven't, try it now. Although this has improved recently, most images you see will nearly all be white men wearing a labcoat. The stereotype of the mad scientist is a hard one to break.

An often-used way of seeing how pupils perceive scientists is to ask them to draw one (see https://en.wikipedia.org/wiki/Draw-a-Scientist_Test). It's very likely that they will mostly draw white men in lab coats and glasses. Some will be bald; some will have crazy hair. Most will look like Einstein, or Doc from Back to the Future. Very few will draw a female or a black scientist.

This very white, very male image of science makes it hard to promote science as something for everyone. Many pupils don't see themselves becoming scientists as they don't see scientists that look like them.

What Pupils Think About Science

A study of pupils by the Wellcome Trust (2019) found that the numbers of pupils who find science interesting, and who thinks they are good at science diminishes over their time in KS2.

Archer et. al (2020) in the Aspires 2 project, looked at young people's science and career aspirations aged 10-14 and found that gender issues are evident from a young age.

Girls are less likely than boys to aspire to science careers, even though a higher percentage of girls than boys rate science as their favourite subject. Once they reach the age of 12-13 years, the research found that 18% of boys and 12% of girls aspire to become scientists; in comparison, 64% of girls aspire to careers in the arts.

Challenge the Stereotypes

Teachers have a responsibility to challenge these stereotypes and present a more diverse image of science. Pupils should feel that a career in science is something that is open to them, whatever their social group or gender. Not all science involves white coats, there are many scientists working in rainforests, deserts and even underwater.

Introduce the pupils to scientists such as Ibn al-Haytham, Marie Curie, George Washington Carver and Stephanie Kvolek to name just a few. There are many great examples of inspiring female scientists in the media such as Professor Alice Roberts, Dr. Helen Czerski, Dr. Maggie Aderin-Pocock and more.

This post explains more: https://www.sciencefix.co.uk/2019/12/raising-interest-and-challenging-stereotypes-in-primary-school-science/

Science Capital

Science capital can be defined as the sum of all the science-related knowledge, attitudes, experiences and resources that an individual builds up through their life. This includes what science they know about, what they think about science, the people they know who have an understanding of science, and the day-to-day engagement they have with science. As teachers, we should consider

This video explains more: https://youtu.be/A0t70bwPD6Y

To do: Listen to the Podcast "How Science Capital can help us address inequalities in STEM Participation". Prof Louise Archer explores how to challenge some of these inequalities in STEM education. Think about what you can do in your science lessons to address this. https://www.ucl.ac.uk/ioe/news/2020/may/how-science-capital-can-help-us-address-inequalities-stem-participation-rftrw-s01e03

Useful Links

Archer, L., Moote, J., MacLeod, E., Francis, B., & DeWitt, J. (2020). ASPIRES 2: Young people's science and career aspirations, age 10-19. London: UCL Institute of Education. https://discovery.ucl.ac.uk/id/eprint/10092041/15/Moote_9538%20UCL%20Aspires%202%20report%20full%20online%20version.pdf

Flynn. S., (2019) Science Literacy. Science Education for Everyday Life. Chartered College https://impact.chartered.college/article/science-literacy-science-education-everyday-life/

Nicholson, D. (2019) Raising Interest and Challenging Stereotypes in Primary School Science. https://www.sciencefix.co.uk/2019/12/raising-interest-and-challenging-stereotypes-in-primary-school-science/

STEM Women: https://www.stemwomen.com/

Science Grrl: https://sciencegrrl.co.uk/

The ASE: What is Science Capital and What does it Look Like in the

Classroom? https://www.ase.org.uk/news/what-science-capital-and-what-does-it-look-in-classroom

Wellcome (2014) Primary Science, Is It Missing Out? https://cms.wellcome.org/sites/default/files/primary-science-is-it-missing-out-wellcome-sep14.pdf

Wellcome (2017) State of the Nation Report of UK Primary Science Education https://cms.wellcome.org/sites/default/files/state-of-the-nation-report-of-uk-science-education.pdf

Wellcome Trust (2019). What Pupils Think of Science in Primary Schools https://cms.wellcome.org/sites/default/files/what-pupils-think-of-science-in-primary-schools.pdf

Printed in Great Britain
by Amazon